RUE TOULOUSE

A French Quarter Fantasy with Marie Laveau, Madame X and an Unwilling Time Traveler

LYNNE JETER

Copyright © 2022 by Lynne Jeter.
All rights reserved.
ISBN: 978-1-955901-19-2

For Cathey Aultman

Table of Contents

Prologue The Grim Reaper..........................1

Chapter 1   Distraught............................. 3
Chapter 2   The Abyss.............................10
Chapter 3   Purgatory.............................12
Chapter 4   The Waiting Place.....................14
Chapter 5   Déjà vu...............................18
Chapter 6   Dread.................................20
Chapter 7   Dormancy.............................. 25
Chapter 8   Revelation............................31
Chapter 9   Spellcasting.......................... 34
Chapter 10   Acclimation.......................... 46
Chapter 11   Backtracking..........................58
Chapter 12   Parker................................ 69
Chapter 13   Currying Favor........................ 78
Chapter 14   Puppet Master.........................91
Chapter 15   Another Ally......................... 114
Chapter 16   Pecking Order........................119
Chapter 17   The Manse............................128
Chapter 18   Battle of Wits.......................134
Chapter 19   Mardi Gras...........................150

Chapter 20 Panic 166
Chapter 21 Dumbfounded 171
Chapter 22 The Day the Earth Stood Still .. 176
Chapter 23 Summoning Damballa 184
Chapter 24 Lacerated Wounds 195
Chapter 25 Tipping Point 204
Chapter 26 Bargaining 208
Chapter 27 Playbook 213
Chapter 28 Play of Shadows Cast 219
Chapter 29 Absolution 235

Epilogue   Curtains 243

Acknowledgements 245

About the Author 247

Prologue

The Grim Reaper

CECILIA ISABELLA BEVILAQUA INTRIGUES ME. Few people have prayed to be whisked away to another netherland like she fervently did. But instead of giving her an easy out, I want to learn more about this tortured soul. I thought she *really* wanted to thrive – simply without dispiriting brawls of rumbling, blackbottomed pain. True, she hasn't had a break in ages.

When she was younger, Cici had a burgeoning personality. She adored life. She praised God. Every morning brought new adventure. I showed up every now and then because she skirted danger more often than she realized. When her dad sent her as a naïve 16-year-old to a seedy part of town to pay loan sharks less than he owed, she could've wound up on the 10 o'clock news.

For a long while, decades really, I lost track of Cici. She seemed to have settled down and started a family and didn't circle my path as often. Now I wonder, as she pleads for death, what happened to push her to the brink? She appears lifeless, isolated, unloved. I almost don't recognize her.

I decide to wait a while. Just to watch and learn. There must be more to the story.

Chapter 1

Distraught

August 12, 2019
927 Rue Toulouse, French Quarter

I HUG THE RUST-STAINED SINK, choking back soul-wrenching sobs at the prospect of my next ill-fated move. I spin the knobs full blast to cover anguished cries. Not long enough ago, a family tragedy ripped apart every fiber of my being, leaving me irretrievably broken. Since then, I've been inconsolable. I may not have the ability to decelerate the gut-punch lashings of life, but I can control the ending, by damn.

Moments earlier, I'd grabbed an arsenal of feel-good and so-called chemical balancing pills that sometimes have the opposite effect. I'd quietly locked the bathroom door, padded lightly on the marble flooring, and with crippled hands that prevent me from doing much that once brought joy, I methodically transform the menagerie of drugs into a dull powdery substance.

I gingerly pick up the Styrofoam cup that contains the toxic sludge and add water.

I blink my eyes, narrow my focus, and consider my dilemma. Could it be this easy to end my wretched life? Or should I use the same tack as my precious daughter?

I press the cup to my lips, hands trembling. Looking into the mirror above the sink, I chastise myself. *Put it down. Don't do it!* Malignant spirits squabble within me. *Come on, you coward! Do it!* My knees wobble. Dizzy and weak, I sink into a crumpled mess on the stone-cold floor, somehow holding the cup steady. What is wrong with me?

I need clarity.

I peer at my reflection. The sparkle in my once-vibrant hazel eyes has long faded. My swollen nose is angry red and overly stuffy; my eyelids are puffy and sticky from dried tears that sully my cheeks and neck. A cardinal flush stains my throat and chest, as if I'm choking on the words I desperately want to say. My olive skin casts a yellowish tinge. My long brunette tresses need a comb-through in the worst way.

I return my gaze to the deadly drink. I steady my trembling hand, tuck a lock of hair behind my ear, and sigh deeply. I'm shivering. Is it from the cold? Or my state of mind? I do *not* want to land in an emergency room and face the aftermath of a failed suicide attempt. This must do the trick. Otherwise, I might be committed to a mental institution. Which, sadly, may be an upgrade.

To distract myself momentarily, I peer on tiptoes through the loft window at the waxing moon before clouds rush to obscure it. Gas lanterns flicker amid sprawling oaks; cool water percolates from myriad fountains. A rare summer breeze tickles musically tuned windchimes and ushers in an enchanting mixture of rose, gardenia, and jasmine blooms. If I listen closely past nature's symphony, I can hear children beating plastic drums for money along Bourbon and a medley of musicians outside Rouse's on Royal. From another street corner, a Creole woman belts out "The House of the Rising Sun." Again.

Briefly, I'm intoxicated by the rare respite and relax my shoulders. Maybe there's hope. Maybe life isn't all bad. The razor-sharp memory of punishing heartbreak could eventually fade, right? Perhaps this cocoon of self-banishment from society is enough to sustain me.

As if on cue, popping sounds punctuate the darkness. Fireworks? Gun shots? The urgency of people scattering indicates the latter. Two weeks ago, two doors down, a twentysomething male waiter at Maison Dupuy, also a part-time Tulane University student, murdered his stepfather, rolled him in a rug, bloody feet sticking out, and held his grandmother hostage. Curious patrons at Fahy's neighborhood bar across the street, who knew something untoward was going on, continued drinking and speculating without fear of being his next victims.

I feel as trapped as the grandmother. Nothing numbs my pain. Not alcohol. Not drugs. Not God, who appears to have gifted me to demons, or else isn't concerned with saving me from them.

Bang! Bang! Bang! Loud rapping on the bathroom door startles me. Parker, my long-suffering husband, demands to know what I'm doing. I struggle to stand up straight.

With door-pounding intensifying, I lift the cup and slurp the poison, winking at myself in the mirror for some foolish reason. It's done now. All that's left is darkness to overtake me. I steady myself and trash the evidence before nonchalantly opening the door. It's a well-practiced façade.

"Yes?"

Parker exhales dramatically. "Cici, I was worried about you."

"I'm ok." Quickly, I change the subject. "Did I hear gunfire?"

"Yeah. Over at Louis Armstrong." The park is a favorite haunt for criminals of all sorts. Pine straw feathering sprawling oaks is littered with used syringes. A safe, picturesque walking trail, it is not.

I change the tone. "I just want to curl up with you."

"I'd love that."

How can I so calmly crush the spirit of a man who remained by my side when we were practically abandoned in our darkest hours?

I crawl into our king-size bed and burrow under my grandmother's wedding ring quilt, my equivalent of a wooby, my version of a Linus blanket. I move my head along Parker's lightly hairy chest until my breathing syncs with the rhythm of his heartbeat. As the room grows quiet, I'm startled by the sight and sound of a black crow at the window. I ignore the superstitious sign for death.

I ponder our life together. Parker remains handsomely strong, witty and with qualities inherent of a "ginger" that draws others to him, even though his hair is mostly gray. A stubborn dark streak remains near the base of his neck. His wideset green eyes crinkle when he gives his charismatic crooked smile.

When we met, I described him as "an English gentleman plucked from the countryside." He would have fit in well at Downton Abbey. I truly, deeply love him, but have nothing left to give. He may even thank me for ending some suffering. I'm a shell of my former self. And a burden. *I'm sorry, Parker. You don't deserve this brand of fate. You'll recover and live a much happier, longer life. Maybe with me out of the picture, your family will return to you.*

As my eyelids grow heavier, I consider the people who lived here before us, in this nearly 200-year-old mansion, in which we have a ridiculously small space. What were they like? How did they live? What trials and tribulations did they endure? How did they overcome adversity?

Or were they also tormented?

Is this place cursed?

Hopefully, the end is near. No more nightmares. No more anguish. No more suffering.

The rabbit hole awaits.

Chapter 2

The Abyss

I'M IN A TUNNEL, but there's no white light. Oddly specifically, it's the Craggy Pinnacle tunnel on the Blue Ridge Parkway near a massive overlook, filling fast with thickening, grayish-black fog. I strain to see signs of life.

Am I dead?

Hazy layers of clouds part enough for me to notice the outline of a familiar figure. I squint. Too far out of my reach, it's my precious daughter who died a year ago. Here, she's very much alive.

I vacillate between the joy of recognizing her and the heartache of realizing her back is turned, arms crossed, in a pouting stance. I call out to her. She doesn't budge.

I'm confused. If I'm dead, she's there to greet me, right? But this isn't a warm reunion.

Am I hallucinating?

Or am I about to delve into the great mysteries of the afterlife? Are heaven and hell all hooey? Does the light flicker out and that's it? Or is there a vast wasteland in between one realm and another?

Is this purgatory?

My eyelids flutter open long enough for me to recognize unprecedented emotional and physical pain. Overwhelmed, I slip back into darkness.

Chapter 3

Purgatory

August 12, 1861
927 Rue Toulouse, French Quarter

A BLAST OF HOT AIR slaps me awake. Why isn't the air conditioner working? A power outage? Has yet another construction crew cut through utility lines?

In complete darkness, I grapple for my wooby. I always keep it within arm's reach. Where is it?

I force my eyes open but cannot focus. My ears are ringing; my stomach roils. Sharp pain overtakes my senses.

I must still be alive.

Dammit.

I cry out to Parker in a whisper.

No response.

"Parker?" I whimper.

Where is he? My chest tightens. What have I done?

Outside, horses whiny. The rhythmic clip-clop of hooves on Rue Toulouse is noisier than usual. More carriages for tourist season? Hmm.

The pulse of the Quarter sounds different. Why am I not hearing incessant honking? Noisy traffic slogs down Rue Toulouse around the clock. Something must've happened. A wreck? Blockade? Another murder? A spontaneous second-line parade?

In the distance, calliope music signals the arrival of a steamboat. A tugboat horn bellows. Powerful air sirens blast the arrival of a train on the riverfront.

I swear I can hear Parker cry out, "Cecilia! Wake up!" But my mind remains a muddled mess. Slumber sinks me once more.

Chapter 4

The Waiting Place

NOISY MUNCHING AND SOUR SMELLS titillate the worn senses. In my loopy state of mind, I imagine floating Cheshire-cat-like in an alternate universe. I laugh. Then I giggle. Until a booming snort jolts me awake.

Peering between partially closed fingers over my eyes, a marvelous, chestnut-colored horse lords over fully vulnerable me. I'm staring at her back end, tail rhythmically swishing. My gut spasms; I sit up straight.

What's happening? Where's my cozy bed? My wooby? Parker, where are you? I need to wake up from this terrible nightmare. I made a mistake! Life *can* get worse.

Slowly, the horse cranes her neck toward me, curls her upper lip, breathes in deeply and blows out hard. Remnants of a sneeze coat the top of my head. With no reaction, she moves to touch me gently with her muzzle, sniffing as if entertained. Her tremendous amber eyes and soulful demeanor somehow make me feel safe and loved.

Trying to calm my high anxiety, I survey my roost. I'm cowering in a dark, dank cubby of a horse stall. Unfamiliar territory, for sure. I love horses but know little about them. Ears pointed backward but not pinned is a good sign, right?

Not trusting the situation or my ignorance of horse body language, I inch away, fearing the weight of hooves on my fragile bones. But in my weakened state, I stumble and plop face down in a puddle of fresh steaming horse dung. The stench prompts me to retch into piled-up hay. Uh-oh, there's blood in my vomit. Not good. I need water.

When the horse lifts her tail, I almost forget to react. I scramble in the opposite direction while the horse releases a steady flow of urine. I shield my face to avoid being splashed. Too late. Worse yet, the seemingly unending waterfall urges my bladder to release. Squatting uncomfortably and holding up my nightgown for some odd sense of decorum, rivulets of bloody pee join the horse's stream.

A gruff, weathered man bellows as he charges toward the stall. A nervous ripple shimmies across the horse's back. As the handler fiddles angrily with grooming gear, the horse turns her head slightly while kicking urine-soaked hay over me as if to keep me safely hidden. I crouch deeper in the corner and spy the horse's name burned into a slab of wood: Zelda Moonshine. I like that. The name suits her gentle yet slightly mischievous nature.

While waiting for the stranger to pass, I do my best to make sense of the disturbing chain of recent events, but throbbing pain breaks my concentration. Rubbing my temples brings no relief. I need my wits about me. Panicking will serve no good. While pinching my nose to minimize the foul odor, I take several deep breaths through my dry mouth. Yuck.

When the coast is clear, an adolescent stable boy moves to calm Zelda, imitating her nicker as if to say, "He's gone. I'll take care of you." It's a practiced routine, and one of comfort for Zelda, who responds by nuzzling his heavily calloused hands.

      Somehow, the groomsman hasn't noticed me.

      But someone else has.

Chapter 5

Déjà vu

IT'S MY FAULT.

I spied a red-headed, pigtailed girl staring dreamily at the pimply-faced groomsman from a half-hidden perch across the courtyard. Crouching like only a child can do, she'd crawled into place after the crochety man departed. The boy appears to be the object of her unrequited affection. A schoolgirl crush.

Unfortunately, my longer-than-should've-been gaze attracts hers. For an uneasy moment, we stare at each other.

The child reminds me of the mean girl, Nelly, from Laura Ingalls Wilder's *Little House on the Prairie*, a spoiled brat constantly stirring trouble. This one wears a fancy outfit for late summer afternoon: an Alice-in-Wonderland pinafore over a chemise, knee-length skirt over posh drawers, *and* pantalettes, all in white.

"Nelly" maintains a stare while shifting awkwardly in clunky, scratched-up shoes. Clearly, I don't belong here.

I flinch first. With a gleam in her eye, she turns on her heels and runs away.

Oh, no! What's she going to do? Who's she going to tell? Should I flee? Even though I'm in unfamiliar territory, instinct tells me to stay put.

Yet, I wonder: what fate awaits me? Where am I? And why do I have the strangest sense of déjà vu?

Chapter 6

Dread

TWILIGHT FALLS FAST. Waves of buffalo gnats, no-see-ums, and "musky toes," better known as mosquitos, feast at dusk. I curl into a fetal position as tightly as possible. Zelda and I quickly learn to peacefully coexist. Exhausted, I drop my head onto wobbly, drawn-up knees.

I really effed up. Badly. I'd pray, but to whom? The reality of abandonment prompts me to tears, but that only worsens the physical torment.

I recall lines from a movie about *Frankenstein* author Mary Shelley: "We both know this is no ghost story," says her friend. "I've never read such a perfect encapsulation of what it feels to be abandoned. I seethed with your monster's rage. I lusted for his revenge. Because it was my own."

I get it now.

Trying to allay the fear that's choking me, I distract myself by looking around the surprisingly lush tropical courtyard centered on a sprawling red oak that looks diminutive, compared to today's 75-footer. Uh-oh.

The garden brims with palm trees and a bamboo grove. Ferns pop out of bricks. Ivy spills over walls. A patchwork of birds brings alive the foliage.

As darkness falls, other sounds emerge. The clanking of pots and pans grows louder, as do footsteps traversing the floor above. Smells of fresh meat pre-marinated in exotic spices and cooking over a fire make my mouth water. I hear sounds of swift hands whipping sauces, scraping bowls, raucous laughter, and chattering in an unfamiliar tongue. Do I hear wolves howling in the distance?

Whispers break the trance.

From the foyer beside the horse stalls, "Nelly" appears with an older woman she calls *Tante* Julie. The French word for aunt. I remember *un peu du Français* from college.

"Nelly" keeps her finger pointed at me far too long.

Julie approaches cautiously while "Nelly" hides behind her aunt's thick layers of gauzy skirts. Tall and thin, using a makeshift cane to balance a limp, Julie appears to be a lovely, gentle woman in her early thirties. Her symmetrical face frames golden brown tendrils twisted into a loose bun, Bohemian-style. But even a sweet smile cannot cover the physical pain she endures with every movement. As a fellow sufferer, I notice the subtleties she's working diligently to conceal.

I remain motionless. Julie stifles a groan as she lowers her body to an uncomfortable crouched position. The irony isn't lost on me: this kind stranger is making more of an effort to help than good friends I thought I could depend on.

"Are you good?"

I shake my head. My chin quivers. Tears flow.

"Tu *vas bien?*" she repeats in French, and then what I later recognize as Creole, perhaps Haitian: "*Eske ou byen?*"

I'm too frightened to respond. Goose bumps crisscross my body.

Julie hesitantly presses the back of her hand to my feces-covered forehead. A few seconds later, she whispers with alarm: "you're burning up!" Startled, she falls backward onto the damp earth, her injured hips taking the brunt of the blow.

She rattles off instructions: "Mimi, quick as you can, go fetch Miz Marie on Saint Ann. Now!"

When I see Mimi close up, she reminds me of my daughter, Izzy. With Julie's urgent orders, she races off. Julie regains her balance.

"There, there, dear," she says soothingly, patting my snotty head. "Poor thing. We'll get you help."

A banging sound startles us.

"Julie! Mimi!" barks a plump woman, banging a copper skillet with a wooden spoon. Birds scatter. The air grows still fast. "Dinner!"

Fanny, as the girls know her, stands with one foot in the foyer and another on the cobblestone. Julie melts into the darkness, undetected. Juggling the skillet and spoon, the woman wipes dirty hands on a blood-stained apron before screeching again: "Dinner!"

Even from a distance, I can tell this unpleasant woman is sweating profusely, bonnet strings flopping around graying wisps of curly red hair. She makes a passable effort of looking in both directions.

"Where are you two?!"

With no response, the woman shouts an empty threat: "Get in here now or else! Madame Avegno won't like you being late – and I'm not taking the blame this time!" While muttering "*imbéciles!*" under her breath, she slams the door.

Julie gives it a minute and reluctantly heads toward the mansion, reassuring me she'll soon return.

Is this all an illusion? Or validation that I'm alive?

Chapter 7

Dormancy

IN THE VAST STILLNESS of the night, illuminated by colossal candle lamps, Zelda continues munching on fresh hay the stable boy pitched into the trough, eyeing me occasionally.

Time drags. Foot traffic has dissipated while dinner is consumed. Zelda shucks the horse blanket off her back, seemingly as a gift of comfort. I use it to wipe my face and hair, then wrap it tightly around me and duck my head. To the casual observer, I simply look like a crumpled rug.

The jangling of silverware and clattering of dishes punctuate the stillness, possibly signaling the switch to dessert. I suppose Julie and Mimi are dining in familial harmony, however forced.

What happened to the rush for help? I don't understand.

Finally, I sense activity. And significant weather change. Fog rolls through the massive iron gate and arched brick carriageway, and sprawls across the courtyard, theatrically announcing the arrival of a curious-looking woman swathed in a fanciful shawl. Dressed in a heavy black muslin blouse and skirt, with hair swept into a seven-point bright gold turban that appears like a crown on her head, the mystery guest looks to be balancing something in both hands.

Julie quietly emerges from the mansion and greets the stranger with ease. They speak in hushed tones. They turn toward Zelda's stall. I can barely make out the words "rough shape ... yellow fever? ... jaundice? ... terribly wrong."

The stranger moves stealthily with a practiced air of distinction. With fog cloaking her entrance, her feet appear to glide across the cobblestones. She's unlike anyone I've ever seen. As she draws closer, I see movement around oversized gold hoop earrings that hit her shoulders. I gasp loudly when I realize it's a light-colored, argyle-patterned corn snake.

I loathe snakes!

Last week, I was crossing Burgundy and Bourbon when I bumped into a man with a corn snake coiled on his shoulder. I'd briefly forgotten it was the staging area for the Bourbon and Toulouse freak show. I instantly retreated, avoiding further incident. When I returned home, Parker schooled me about corn snakes. At first glance, they mimic the venomous copperhead. But they're commonly kept as pets because of their docile nature, reluctance to bite, and simple care.

"Don't be afraid. This is Le Grand Zombi," the stranger says in a deep, husky voice. "He's named after an African god. We call him Zombi."

I gulp. Julie assures me it's safe.

"When I carry Zombi," explains the stranger, "nobody bothers me."

Up close, she's luminous. Her topaz eyes glimmer like precious jewels. I surmise her smooth mahogany, freckled skin is an exotic mix of black, white, and perhaps Indian blood. Is she mulatto? Creole? I could never understand the subtle differences, having grown up in a Deep

South black-and-white world during the turbulent Civil Rights movement.

In her left hand, she holds a gourd rattle trained on Zombi. When she touches my shoulder with her right hand, I feel a slight shock, a ripple of warm energy shooting through my body. Her golden turban glows.

"Where'd you come from, dear?"

I blink, tongue-tied. She pushes the back of her hand on my forehead and holds it a few seconds.

"We'd have nothing to do with you if you have yellow fever, but your fever isn't high enough and you're not vomiting black gunk or bleeding from your eyes," she speaks, authoritatively. I remember reading about outbreaks of yellow fever in the mid-1800s that wiped out 10 percent of the city's population. "I need you to cooperate with us before we can help you. You want help, right?"

With no response, the stranger turns to Julie, speaking rapidly in a language I don't understand. If the stranger hadn't turned sideways, I might not have recognized the famous profile – overarching painted brows, slender nose, small ears, and unnaturally full lips. Why does she look familiar?

Losing patience, she leans forward, eyes narrowing, and asks as a statement: "Where. Did. You. Come. From."

I say nothing; exhaustion has dampened my wit.

It occurs to me that I first noticed her printed image at the foot of the Saint Louis Cathedral. Fortune tellers popping up card tables between the church and Jackson Park talked incessantly about this woman. *Instant recall, where are you?*

While trying to place the stranger, I reluctantly register a more significant fact. Evidence has been piling up about the timeline of the Madame X mansion – stables instead of an apartment, a kitchen in lieu of another, historical costumes usually seen only in plays, during Carnival season or Halloween.

I groan as the awful truth reveals itself.

I'm in the same place, but *not* the same time.

"What ... um ... time is it?" I whisper, weakly.

"It's probably close to 9 o'clock," Julie says, calculating the darkness.

"No, I mean, what time period?"

With a furrowed brow, Julie speaks haltingly: "What time period ... do you think it is?"

I shrug my shoulders.

From the telltale signs, and assuming I'm not in some historically recreated venue like Colonial Williamsburg, I venture a guess. "Um ... the mid-1800s?"

In a hushed tone of disbelief, Julie whispers "Yes."

Chapter 8

Revelation

I'M WEIRDLY CERTAIN of the stranger's identity. It all makes sense in a twisted, sordid way.

I'm staring at a purveyor of the dark arts, known for incantations and curses, magnanimous deeds, and mysterious deaths. Gamblers shout her name while tossing dice. Admirers flock to her grave and seek her spirit through seances. Some read Tarot cards in her honor. Many have sworn ghostly sightings of her in the form of a black cat. Or a black crow, depending on the storyteller.

During her heyday, this Louisiana Creole herbalist and midwife, who masqueraded as a hairdresser while bartering in gossip, had the goods on every major player in New Orleans' high society, especially political circles. She kept an enviable network of collaborators of taboo secrets and fabricated lies while practicing rootwork, Native American and African spiritualism.

She's the Crescent City's most celebrated Voodoo Queen. Modern day, she's a rock star.

"You're … you're … you're …," I stammer and point weakly. I tap my forehead with my fingers to help stoke my memory.

Both women exchange glances seeking clues about my mental state. Julie disappears briefly to fetch metallic-tasting water. I swallow too hard and fast. After a coughing fit, I try again.

I force the words to form on my tongue.

"You're … you're …" I've rarely had such trouble talking.

After a pause, and with great effort and surprising confidence, I blurt out: "You're Marie Laveau!"

"What?" Julie gasps and steps back.

The stranger scoffs, striking a pose by craning her swan-like neck to size up the situation. Long, lean fingers curl around a cypress cane sculpted in the shape of a serpent, exposing dagger-like nails. Zombi dances across her shoulders. Wolves howl in the distance. Or are they werewolves? My imagination gets the better of me. I resist the urge to say more.

After an awkward beat, Marie moves uncomfortably close to my face, the snake near enough to strike, and speaks in a deep, measured tone that terrifies me to the core.

"How ... do you ... know me?"

The weight of trauma washes over me. I slump forward until the world turns black. Again.

Chapter 9

Spellcasting

I VAGUELY REMEMBER shuffling sounds and groans as the stable boy lifts me into his arms.

"Be careful, Ollie. She's in awful shape," Julie fusses.

The groomsman cradles me as the trio shuffle awkwardly toward a side door. Julie hobbles ahead while Marie Laveau stalks the shadows. I jump when buckets of cistern water are poured over my head in some semblance of cleaning me up before taking me inside. Ollie grimaces at the blast of cold water.

Holding open the door, Julie steps onto the polished mahogany staircase and points to the second floor. Ollie redistributes my body weight and holds me tightly as we climb to Julie's bedroom.

They're counting on me to remain quiet. Ollie gently places me on Julie's soft bed. With a softly lit candle, Marie moves swiftly to study me, handing Zombi to an ill-prepared Ollie. Scowling, he contains the wiggly creature in both hands like a spool of yarn.

"What's that?" Marie asks rhetorically, spying a Band-aid in the crook of my right arm. I'd had blood drawn the day before. Marie cautiously lifts my tattered, cotton voile gown to inspect my legs, rubbing a finger over a tattoo on my right ankle. She's intrigued by the nail polish on my toenails. She gently pries open my mouth to check for gold. I close my eyes. Candle wax drips onto my cheek.

Marie's intense gaze is unsettling. She leans forward and speaks in a calculated tone: "Tell me, child, where did you come from? And how do you know me?"

Marie retrieves Zombi from Ollie, who Julie ushers quickly out the door. I hear whispers of "thank you" and "won't tell" before Julie quietly closes the door. Both took significant risks for me because in those days, it's unacceptable for an unmarried male to be seen leaving an unmarried lady's room.

When I try to rise on my elbows, Marie gently presses on my left shoulder, insisting I remain still. She dispatches Julie to fetch herbs – bitterroots, chamomile, laurel leaves, moss, orange leaves, potato leaves and sassafras, or whatever combination she can find on short notice – to bring down my fever and address my internal injuries. While Zombi dances like a halo around Marie's head, she continues examining me. I squirm.

Marie demands answers: "Who are you? And where did you come from?"

What should I tell her? Nobody will believe me. I wouldn't believe me. I'm cornered. I decide to say as little as possible.

I stammer: "I'm ... I'm ... Cecilia." My voice trails off; she asks my name again.

"Cici for short, ma'am," I reply, respectfully.

"Ma'am? Why you call me ma'am? I ain't your ma'am!" Marie rolls her eyes.

I'd forgotten that social faux pas. While ma'am- today is prevalently regarded as a sign of respect, in the mid-1800s, it was reserved to address the lady of the house. I mentally kick myself. How will I get out of this situation?

Marie points to the bandage on my arm.

"I've never seen anything like it," she speaks in a gravelly tone.

I slowly peel off the Band-Aid to expose a red dot of blood pooled around the needle insertion site. "I gave blood," I explain, rather awkwardly.

Marie points to my nails. "Nail polish," I explain. Was anyone using nail polish back then?

She notes my tattoo cloaked in Mardi Gras green, stately purple and golden yellow.

"It's a butterfly," I whisper with effort, and then joke, "Ready to fly away." Zombi seems fascinated with my voice. He teasingly flicks his tongue and moves mesmerizingly about Marie's neck.

Marie says nothing. I squirm again.

Marie leans forward and asks again, deliberately: "How ... do ... you ... know ... me?"

I gulp. Then I notice something odd. Marie doesn't seem surprised.

Julie's return mercifully cuts short the uncomfortable lull in conversation.

"Here, have some tea," Julie says, handing me a cup and saucer filled with putrid-smelling liquid.

"What kind is this?" I ask suspiciously, in a raspy voice that clearly needs lubrication. Normally, I would've followed the question with: "Oolong? Earl Grey?" But I discipline myself to say nothing further.

I take a small sip and spew it over Julie, Marie and Zombi.

"I'm sorry," I mutter, retreating under the bed covers. "It's ..." I don't want to insult my hostess, but I cannot bear to swallow more, no matter how parched my throat.

Marie cackles; Zombi's eyes gleam.

"It's medicine," Marie explains. "You need it for what ails you."

"What about antibiotics?" I blurt out. "Or Tylenol?" Doh.

Marie and Julie exchange puzzled looks.

"Antibiotics. Drugs that make you well," I try to explain. "Tylenol, for headaches."

I'm speaking badly-timed gibberish. Paul Ehrlich won't deliver the first antibiotic until 1907, to treat syphilis.

"You'll take what we give you," Marie commands. I weakly acquiesce and swallow a few sips with great effort.

"Do you have bread?" I ask, hoping to neutralize the bitter residue.

Julie slips outside the room in search of a morsel. Once the door clicks shut, Marie presses again. "Ok, sissy, we're alone again. I'll ask you once more: how do you know me?"

I feverishly search my mind for a suitable answer.

"I ... I ... I fell asleep in my bed," I start. "But ... I woke up in a barn. I don't understand ..."

Surprisingly, Marie warms to me. "Tell me more. What did you do before you went to sleep?"

She knew. Or did she? Paranoia consumes me.

"I ... um ... took some pills ..." my voice trails off.

"Laudanum? Is that it?"

Laudanum? Oh yes, poison.

"Something like that."

"But it didn't take ...?"

"I guess not. Unless I'm dead. Or in purgatory. Is this the waiting place?"

"No, child. You've traveled far," she responds, adjusting a hoop earring as Zombi changes direction. "In your mind."

"What?"

"Yours hasn't been a journey across miles," she continues. "You've crossed another plane. A different time."

I furrow my brow. "What do you mean, another time?"

"Do you know what year it is?"

I shake my head.

"Guess," she teases.

I don't like this game.

I search the room for clues. I peg the years between 1859 and 1867, based on the state of clothing and furnishings. The upstart of the Civil War meant saving money. Bodices and petticoats weren't cleaned as often; some hems had frayed slightly. It seems to be in the early stages, so I guess 1861. I remember the blistering month.

"August 1861?"

Marie gasps. Her eyes narrow as she absorbs this new truth. I'd arrived four months after the start of the Civil War. She leans forward again, this time quite animated.

"How do you know, child?"

I shrug.

Julie's arrival again breaks the spell. She smiles sweetly as she hands me fresh bread, pinching off a bite. "Don't eat it fast. It'll upset your balance."

Balance? That's a new one.

"Thank you," I manage. I'm in that crazy state of feeling starved, yet also repulsed by food. I nibble steadily. Dare I say it's the most delicious bread I've ever had?

While I eat, Marie and Julie discuss my situation as if I'm not here. Both fall into a heavy Creole dialect that communicates nothing to me.

"*C marche comme un papier de musique*," Marie told Julie, which I later learned means "there's no trouble; everything's going smoothly."

Suddenly, the conversation stops, and both turn to me.

"Ok, you'll stay here with Julie," Marie decides. "I'll check on you when I come do

Madame's hair tomorrow. Get some rest. We have a lot to do to get you well."

I'm relieved.

Julie nods as she grabs light blankets and a chamber pot. "You stay in bed. I'll sleep on the floor."

"No," I protest, like a well-mannered southern girl. "You need your bed."

"You need it more."

I weakly agree. "But just for the night." I'm unaccustomed to such hospitality.

Marie addresses my health while getting up to leave. "Ok, sissy. You gone be alright. What you took didn't damage you much. If you'd added liquor, you'd be dead. But you're going to need time to recover. And we've got to figure out what to do with you."

Marie instructs Julie to make a potion for kidney trouble, after noticing blood stains from vomiting and, she deduced correctly, in my urine and poop. "We need swamp-lily root to crush and steep in a quart of water. She'll need to drink it all.

"Also, she's complaining of a headache. Hang a string with nine knots around her neck. That should cure it."

Before parting, Marie abruptly spits on my forehead, spouts gibberish, and crosses her heart.

"Marie cast a spell on you for safekeeping," Julie explains.

Should I wipe it off? Or let it linger? My knowledge of spellcasting is greatly limited.

Julie opens the door slightly to let Marie slip by and presses her ear to the wall until footsteps pass and the halls are quiet. It wouldn't seem terribly inappropriate for Marie to visit this time of night. She's always helping those who are sick or need potions of some sort. But it would raise eyebrows. Marie's primarily a day guest, only there to service the lady of the house, the "ma'am." And to increase her importance in the underground network.

After stoking the fire, Julie slumps into a rocking chair. Her kindness softens the blow of presenting a most curious yet dreaded and disturbing question. Leaning toward me, pressing her hand gently on my arm, she asks softly:

"What's your story?"

Again, I'm speechless. What can I say? That my life has fallen completely apart in ways I could never have foreseen? Who would understand any of it? I certainly don't. Thinking about my pathetic situation draws tears.

Upon seeing my distress at the inability to come up with a response, Julie squeezes my hand.

"Don't worry. We'll discuss it later. Get some rest."

Chapter 10

Acclimation

I STIR TO THE SOUNDS and smells of a lavish breakfast being made across the hall. Instantly, I'm ravenous. I'm also alone. And I hurt all over. But I'm also grateful for a decent night's rest. At one point, I woke briefly when I thought I heard my name called. Oh, how I wish it was Parker! Where is he? I miss him terribly. What was I thinking? What have I gotten myself into? I sigh deeply.

My impatient, overactive bladder overwhelms my attention. Where's that chamber pot? My stomach spasms. *Pain, stop!* Whatever concoction Marie mixed seems to have helped. I could be dead. I'm unconvinced I'm not in limbo.

Fetching the pot from underneath the bed, I wonder: do you squat over it? It's mighty small. Will it run over? That would be unpleasant. I finally wiggle and squirm until I hit my target. Relief washes over me. Now what? Toilet paper had entered the market in 1857, marketed as "Gayetty's Medicated Paper for the Water-Closet"—500 sheets for 50 cents – but isn't yet mainstreamed. Struggling to maintain an uncomfortable position, I shake my booty until few droplets remain. Talk about an ab crunch. Ugh!

With that chore done, I peruse the space. Julie has two rooms on the third floor that run deep and narrow. Not wanting to tip off movement on creaky wooden floors to the master suite below, I tiptoe into the second room, Julie's studio, overlooking the magnificent courtyard. Several easels hold works in varying stages of progress, mostly depicting objects in nature. Some are colorful; others are sad shades of gray. I notice there's a small timeframe for optimal light in the room. I remember that limitation from times I painted in my "spare" room downstairs.

I can imagine that, in good weather, Julie takes her work outdoors. But as is often the case in the French Quarter, rain is an afternoon constant companion in late summer. The bottom falls out without warning, leaving a sultry, steamy aftermess. Despite limitations, I marvel at her setup. No easy-to-squeeze oil paints here. She must carefully combine colors from natural ingredients. How spoiled I've been to order Winton oil paint tubes at $3.49 each from Jerry's Artarama that delivers supplies in two days, free shipping.

I return to the first room. Except for a squeaky floorboard I now know to avoid, I move surprisingly silently. A wardrobe sits in a dark corner, holding everyday dresses, all in white, and a slightly faded evening gown in purple silk. A massive trunk sits at the end of the bed. A dressing table and oversized floor mirror flank the wardrobe. I imagine Julie sitting down to brush and then braid her long, silky hair. I guess she often bypasses the option "to paint her face," a decision that angers her snobby high-society sister, Mimi's mother. Oh, yes, vanity is Madame Virginie Avegno's most obvious deadly sin of choice.

A small writing desk rests in front of a tall window that offers little insulation. Cards and letters are stacked in an ornate, cream-colored French Provincial box with gold lettering. Nearby sits an ink jar, quill pens and fine velum white paper. Calling cards are scattered loosely in a corner of the desk, with Julie's name printed in calligraphy.

I've read varying accounts about Julie, the younger daughter of the irascible, domineering, narcissistic Marie Virginie Ternant Parlange. Julie has been treated poorly in the family since dodging the marriage of Lieutenant Lucas Rochilieu, a greasy looking, much older, obese French aristocrat with hair sprouting in all the wrong places. He planned to carry her away to his family's compound and already made clear he wanted many children.

Julie's mother had "sold" her hand in marriage in exchange for enough money to keep the family's fledgling plantation going another year. For a brief while, the estate, with 10,000 acres of farmland bordering the interestingly named False River, made Marie Virginie the area's richest and most powerful landowner and harvester of cotton, indigo and sugar cane. She couldn't bear to lose it. At any cost.

Here's what happened: Julie was unhappy about being manipulated. Just the thought of her fiancé, with a nasty mole on the tip of his nose, climbing on top of her made her ill. Plus, he had a bandage covering an ugly, seepy wound over an eye from accidentally shooting himself while cleaning his gun months earlier. If he represented the family image, relatives would surely be unpleasant: optional manners and self-care barbaric. If she went through with the marriage, she would be at their beck and call. Her freedom would end abruptly. Painting would not be permissible. Her life, and all that she loved about it, would wither until a wished-for premature death.

The morning of her wedding, Julie dressed in a heavy cream satin ball gown, her lustrous hair swept into a tidy bun dotted with pink rosebuds that wilted quickly in the heat. In a moment of despair, she begged her mother to stop the wedding. Marie Virginie scoffed at, and emphatically denied, her request. Rochilieu was awaiting his bride downstairs in a starched white shirt, pinstriped brown trousers, and a Prince Albert frock coat garnished with a lapel cameo stickpin.

Heartsick, Julie paced across the broad-planked cypress floor carrying rosary beads, reciting prayers non-stop, occasionally gazing at the river, a picturesque lagoon formed from a bend in the Mississippi River that surrounded the two-story raised cottage. In a moment of clarity, Julie defiantly dropped the beads, strode to the second-floor balcony of the French colonial plantation house, grabbed a fistful of cream satin to her hips with one hand and a white column with the other.

Julie clumsily stepped onto the railing in sleek white slippers and stared upward to the sky. Spreading her wings like an angel, she managed a swan dive toward a tremendous oak on the terraced lawn, her dress billowing like a failed parachute. Landing flat on her face in the lush green grass, Julie appeared motionless. Everyone feared the worst. When turned over, Julie's face was bluish-white and her body limp. But she had a pulse. Maybe.

Julie's half-brother, Charles, rushed her to a neglected bedroom. He was sweating profusely in stiff white linen garments and mumbling how the heat must've driven her mad. Marie Virginie didn't want the bridegroom to know what had happened. Instead, she told him Julie had died, wailing histrionically to great effect. Soon after, the bridegroom fled the estate in a fit of fury. When he was out of sight, the staff raised a white towel on a pole at the front gate, indicating the need for a doctor visit on his daily rounds.

After several agonizing hours, Julie's color returned to her cheeks and her fingers trembled uncontrollably. Julie would live after all. But both legs were broken. She suffered several cracked ribs and a damaged spine, leaving her an invalid for months, and crippled for life. Still, she seemed to prefer permanent disability to the marriage of "a beast" she called "simply wretched."

Julie's plight cast a shadow over her family. For many years, Marie Virginie allowed rumors to bear fruit of

Julie's death, even planting the seeds of a wedding-day ghost circling Parlange Plantation House. When Julie's behavior became erratic, Marie Virginie didn't hesitate to send her to an asylum for a time-out. Other speculation indicates Marie Laveau collaborated with a local pharmacist on experimental drugs for Julie's malady and depression.

Regardless, it makes sense for Julie to want to save a fellow sufferer.

Hearing scratching noises outside the door, I clamber back into bed. Just as I pull the cover over my shoulders, Julie enters cheerfully with a plateful of sliced oranges and freshly baked muffins, spiced with cinnamon, currants, and nuts. Once I settle into an upright position, she hands me a glass of dark juice. I nod gratefully and dig in. It's so delicious. The juice, on the other hand, seems to be made of prunes without sugar. My lips pucker to Julie's amusement.

"It'll help move your meals," she says, with a smile.

I'll bet. Prune juice has always worked fast on my digestive system. I want to be prepared. I search for the chamber pot, wondering where I should pour the contents. As if reading my mind, Julie scoops up the full chamber pot and in a solid, fluid motion, tosses the urine into the courtyard. I gasp. No wonder people died from all sorts of maladies. The routine makes me terribly uncomfortable. How will the second pot, the poopy one, be emptied?

"That goes into the street, not the courtyard," Julie says, again reading my thoughts. "That's why men and women carry umbrellas, no matter the weather."

While I eat, Julie studies me. On one hand, I could be a stranger who poses danger. On the other, I could be a kindred spirit to fill the monotonous void in her life. Or I might be a combination of the two.

Chapter 11

Backtracking

I AWAKE FROM TROUBLED, pained sleep long enough to remember the plight that landed me here. I miss the white noise from the desk fan that lulls me to sleep. I miss air conditioning. Truth be known, I wish I'd succeeded with my death wish. I was almost disappointed when my fever returned to normal. A high fever would finish the job I started, wouldn't it? Remembering the timeline of when life soured brings me to tears. Julie stirs when I sniff. I take several deep breaths to calm myself.

I cannot recall the exact moment everything went amiss. Was it during our daughter's formative years? Did I miss something important along the way? Or during her college days? Or post-graduation when her life was truly starting?

Since the "incident," I insist on calling it, I've second-guessed every decision made during our daughter's lifetime.

Boom! A thunderous sound disrupts my troubled thoughts. Julie stirs but remains asleep. I peer out the window to determine the source. The skies are clear. Then I recall my history lessons. With talk of another yellow fever epidemic blowing through New Orleans, Creole men fire cannons into the still night air "to destroy germs," despite the danger it presents during wartime. Fortunately, Union soldiers are not yet prevalent.

Night air, I'd heard, was the dreaded culprit for spreading disease. Burning juniper berries indoors was highly encouraged to "sanitize" the air. Windows, even on the most unforgivingly miserable summer evenings, remain tightly shut. Oh, the irony that each bedroom has a fireplace and therefore some ventilation.

I settle under the covers and continue the cycle of awkward reflections.

After believing it was too late for us, Parker and I gave birth to a strawberry-blonde daughter, Isabelle. Izzy, as we called her, had an angelic face with sharp blue eyes, cherry lips, high cheekbones and, an odd ingredient for a fair-haired girl, my Mediterranean skin. She had Parker's high forehead, rounded eyebrows, and gregarious personality. The genes blended well.

As a child, she was always laughing, singing, and finding new ways to bring us joy. She was a delight to raise, rarely causing problems. She kept her mischievous streak under wraps better than we did. She was the best of us, but sadly, shared our temper. On rare occasions, her disposition was anger on steroids. Fortunately, she learned to tame it.

She was smart and loved to go head-to-head with her dad over social issues. They were so close; we were all remarkably close. That's why after Izzy endured a deeply traumatizing rape, we were completely helpless about her decision to end it all the way she did.

The body does funny things when blasted with tragic news. When I learned Izzy was dead, my knees buckled and I fell to the floor until my cheek rested on wooden planks. Some unknown magnetic force pulled me what seemed like three feet under. I never fully recovered from that blow. Parker remains haunted by the pitiful, moaning cries I made, a mother mourning her child. Every morning, even now, I awake with one thought: What could I have done differently for a different outcome?

The news bowled over Parker. His eyes stayed red for days, weeks if I'm honest. We were both inconsolable, yet we couldn't console each other. We had clashing ways how to deal with her void, and all I wanted was to get away from him. Just for a few hours. Ok, maybe a few days. No longer than a week. I'd miss him too much. But he also reminded me too much of Izzy.

We didn't get that break and it almost did us in. We were hanging by a flimsy thread to sanity and each other.

A round of three short knocks followed by the doorknob turning of Julie's door broke my concentration. Julie jumps, still woozy. Thank goodness she had locked the door tightly. No one can get in without a key. She has one; the main housekeeper has the other. Footsteps pad away and then return. This time, the trio of knocks is followed by the turning of a key. Julie rushes to the door. Behind it, Mimi hurries to see me.

"Are you feeling better?" she asks, enthusiastically.

"Yes, I am. Thank you for asking, sweetie."

"My name's Amelie, but my friends call me Mimi," she says. "I haven't been called 'sweetie' before."

"It's a term of endearment," I explain. "It means I think a lot of you!"

Mimi smiles broadly.

"What do you want, Mimi?" Julie asks, a tad impatiently.

"Just to see how Cici's doing. There's a lot of excitement in the house today. Mama is happy for a change. She wouldn't be happy to find a stranger right under her nose."

"Well, then, off you go," Julie directs Mimi to the door. As Mimi departs, another person taps on the door. My heart races. Have we been caught? Julie whispers a few words, firmly closes the door, and locks it.

"Don't worry," she reassures me. "That was word from Marie that she'll be here at lunchtime to fix Virginie's hair. She'll come see you right after."

Then Julie leaves the room, leaving me to my melancholy.

Memories flood again about my pitiful life. I remember the night Izzy came home, bleeding and bawling. She'd decided to walk to The Bienville House on Rue Decatur to meet friends at its cozy bar at 6 o'clock. It was the dead of winter and daylight was short. We knew there were a couple of dark areas along the route. It was a rainy, warmish night. We tried to talk her out of wearing a super cute skater dress that accentuated her lean legs, but there was a guy who interested her, and we didn't blame her for wanting to look sexy.

To get there, she could take Rues Burgundy, Dauphine, Bourbon, Royal, or go straight to Rue Decatur, and then right. From the northeast, taking any of the remaining four streets traversed Rues Saint Louis, Conti, Bienville, and Iberville. I thought she should go straight down Rue Decatur. Parker thought she should stroll down Rue Bourbon to Rue Iberville to catch Rue Decatur, where crowds gathered.

From what we could tell from her sobbing, she took Rue Toulouse to Rue Burgundy, past Fahy's Bar, so she could chat with Iko, a most fascinating 20-year-old parrot. Sometimes, he's a priest in a confessional. People tell Iko their deepest, darkest fears. Drunken tourists encourage him to dance on the cage, or "talk." His hippie mistress encourages him to do tricks when money is tight; the tip jar usually overcomes any shortfall. After you get to know Iko, you realize tourists annoyed him, complainers bored him, and he only spoke to a chosen few. He loved Izzy and let her stroke his feathers.

How did I get so far off track? Maybe because I don't want to go there. It was a dreadful night. Izzy stumbled in the kitchen door, ready to collapse. Her frizzy hair was wet. Her clothes were soaked. Her rain jacket was torn. She was cold, almost blue. Then I noticed bodily fluids streaming down her legs and I knew. She had been raped. We were both holding each other when Parker came into the room. I watched him glance over her, and his eyes linger on her thighs. He knew, too, and it made him sick. We guided her to the bathroom, where we listened helplessly to her moans emanating from the bottom of the shower. She refused to report the rape, knowing the rape kit experience added insult to injury. She knew thousands of rape kits sat untested on police shelves across the country. We could do nothing but love her.

When she was calmer, Izzy recounted the nightmarish experience. A hooded man had jumped her when she turned down Rue Conti, shoved her into an iron gate with a protruding doorknob, thrust a gun to her forehead and took what little cash she had in her pocket. Instead of letting her go, he spun her around and raped her, the doorknob bruising her stomach with every movement. Ironically, she was a few doors down from what used to be the mid-1900s "boarding house" at 1026 Conti of Norma Wallace, the Last Madam of New Orleans. Even though the former brothel had been turned into apartments, and she screamed at the top of her voice, no one tried to save her. It's strange the little things one remembers during a traumatic experience. On the long way home, she noticed a sign designating the street as Calle D Conti between 1762 and 1803, when New Orleans was capitol of the Spanish Province of Louisiana.

Over months, we sought silver linings to tamp down the grief we couldn't swallow. One and two, he was a small man and oddly gentle. A larger, rougher man would have done even more physical damage. Three, he was a quick comer. He orgasmed within a minute and didn't try anal sex. Four, he was alone. It could've been a gang rape. Five, she didn't get pregnant. That was one to watch for weeks because the rape occurred when she was ovulating and not on birth control. We can only suspect that he withdrew somewhat, or that her uterus was fortunately inhospitable to him.

Also, she was embarrassed about possibly being seen by others on the street, or heaven forbid being videotaped by some voyeur, wishing instead for some modicum of modesty.

But we were only fooling ourselves. Nothing was good about her ordeal. The experience haunted her, especially at night. Watching her struggle was excruciating. The image of being raped and mugged faded some with time. But she could never get over the emotional shredding of the fabric of her being. We encouraged her to find a counselor. We'd gladly pay. We'd do joint counseling if she preferred. But she couldn't even work. She moved in with us to cut costs. We were glad to keep an eye on her. But none of it mattered in the end. On a sultry summer evening a year ago, August 12 to be exact, with a waning crescent moon hovering over the city, Izzy walked out of 927 Rue Toulouse and jackknifed off the Mississippi River Bridge.

It's little wonder I prayed for death nightly. Suicidal ideation took precedence in my thought patterns. One idea was to take a fistful of sleeping pills, smoke a doobie, maybe down straight vodka, put on something slutty, and take a stroll. That was the plan: to simply walk around the French Quarter unprotected and vulnerable. Then I could feel what Izzy felt. And a bonus if I ended up dead. Let someone else do the dirty work.

Before I could conjure up more ways to end my life, my health began failing spectacularly. I had a laundry list of problems. During that one-year period, I had a half dozen surgeries, each time praying before the anesthesia set in that I wouldn't awake. Life held no interest. All these horrible stitches of suffering led to the near-death experience that occurred less than 24 hours ago.

Suddenly, I want to live. I want to be home with Parker. I'll work on my issues harder to get better quicker. I'm willing to negotiate almost anything to return to some semblance of normal.

Chapter 12

Parker

WHILE I STRUGGLE to come to terms with the damage I've done—to my body, my spirit, and Parker – he is deciding what to do with me.

"Cecilia, wake up!" Parker cries in anguish. In the bed beside him is my ostensibly lifeless body. After fumbling for some time, he detects a pulse. He's relieved but confused.

"Cici! Cici!" I do not respond. I'm living a double life he cannot comprehend. He knows something profound is going on as my eyes briefly show signs of REM sleep, darting back and forth under closed eyelids. He's panicked at the twitching in my face and irregular breathing.

Maybe she's in a deep slumber, Parker reconciles. She'll come out of it, right? After all, REM sleep is the last stage before waking, isn't it? In the meantime, I must know what she's done, so I'll know how to help her.

Parker races to the bathroom and scours the wastebasket. I didn't make it easy for him to find evidence. He digs under used tissues and dental floss until he finds the empty Styrofoam cup, rubs his finger along the inner rim, then licks it for clues.

"What has Cici done?" he asks aloud. He moves to the kitchen trashcan, where, after more burrowing, he finds as assortment of pill shells. At best count, there are 52. How can she not be dead?

Parker returns to my side and checks my vitals again. How had he missed signs of my deep depression? How did he not know what I'd been planning? He picks up the phone and dials my best friend, who answers right away.

"Rachel, Cici isn't waking up. I think she overdosed. Has she talked to you lately?"

Rachel is taken aback. "Oh, no! She hasn't called me lately, though I knew she'd been quite despondent. I should've checked on her more often."

"I didn't know it was that bad, either. She's been keeping to herself a lot lately."

"Has she been painting?" Rachel knew that was my way of coping.

"Not really. She worked on a couple of canvases and threw them away. She wishes she could do better and gets frustrated. But I don't think that put her over the edge," Parker waves his arms melodramatically to an audience of none.

"No, but it shows her state of mind," notes Rachel. "Nothing has worked out for that poor soul. I've never seen anyone so tormented. What are you going to do?"

"I don't want to take her to an emergency room. No telling what they'd do to her. She doesn't seem in immediate distress, but something's wrong, terribly wrong. I can feel it."

"What about her mother? Have they talked lately?"

"She won't tell her mother anything anymore. She's still deeply hurt by her mother's response to Izzy's death. Remember, she's a staunch southern Baptist who fully believes those who commit suicide rot in hell."

"Other than you and me, she has no one to turn to," Rachel laments. "That's sad. We're not equipped to help someone with as many problems as she has."

"I know, but I should've seen her despair." This time, he means. I'd flirted with death on various occasions, but always softball tries. Mainly, I wanted a break from life that never came.

After a pause, Parker remembers a friend we have in common, a new pal we'd made the acquaintance of recently in the Quarter: a veterinarian. He's not a medical doctor, but he would do in a pinch.

"What do you think?" Parker asks Rachel. "He's the only one I trust to look at her and not say anything."

"Give it a try. It's better than nothing. Keep me posted."

After hanging up, Parker debates what to tell the veterinarian and decides it must be truthful. He maneuvers the cell phone directory and finds Dr. Barkley's contact info. Should he call? Text? Or walk to his place five blocks toward the river?

Parker studies my body, no longer in REM sleep but, despite his best efforts, also no closer to waking/ up. He dials Barkley's number; he answers on the fourth ring.

"Oh, hello, Parker, how's Molly?" Barkley asks, referencing our aging golden retriever.

"Hi, Dr. Barkley. No, it's not about Molly. This is about my wife. She's, um, not waking up. She ... took some pills. But she has a pulse."

"Why aren't you calling 9-1-1?"

"I don't want some medical team to start messing with her and send her away to some mental institution," Parker confides. "She's been through enough already."

"Is there not a doctor you can call? Does she not have a primary care physician?"

"We haven't been here long enough to find one we trust."

For a moment too long, Barkley says nothing. Then, he reluctantly agrees to come over.

"Make sure you're looking for me, so you can ring me in. I don't want to be left standing at the gate."

To save my dignity, Parker cleans me up. He changes me out of my nightgown, accidentally ripping part of a sleeve while taking it off. Perhaps that's the reason why my cotton gown in 1861 was partially tattered? It was made in China, after all. Not well sewn. He finishes redressing me when the front door rings. Instead of Barkley, it's our next-door neighbor, Bill, wondering if we need anything on a run to Rouse's on Royal.

"No, we're good," Parker says, a bit too dismissively. "Thank you, though."

"Hey, maybe later, we'll get together in the courtyard," Bill says, encouragingly. "Tell Cici we've got some new stuff to try."

"Sounds good," Parker says, trying to wrap up the conversation. He knows "stuff" is code for marijuana. Cici would've liked that. A good hit usually dulls her senses – and her memory –for a little while, at least. Fortunately, our neighbor leaves rather quickly.

A minute later, the doorbell rings again. It's Barkley. Parker buzzes him in right away.

"Thank you for coming. I know I'm putting you in a bad spot," Parker says, appreciatively.

"No problem. I just hate to hear something's wrong with Cici."

Parker escorts Barkley to our bedroom. "I'll leave you alone with her. Let me know if you need anything."

After a few minutes, Barkley walks into the kitchen and finds Parker cleaning the countertop out of nervousness.

"Parker, the best I can tell is that Cici has slipped into a light coma," he reports, yet isn't sure how to calculate her range on the Glasgow Coma Scale without medical equipment. "I don't think she needs to go to an emergency room, at least not yet. But if you want to keep her home, and I understand why you do, you'll need an eagle eye on her. I'll be on standby if you need me. Now, during the day at my practice, it may take me a little while to get back to you. But if it's urgent, text 9-1-1 and I'll drop everything."

"Thank you, Dr. Barkley. How do I keep her hydrated and fed?"

"I'm going to make it easy for you by sending over a nurse to insert a feeding tube," he says. "Her name is Allison and she's a pro. She'll have all the supplies you need. She'll teach you how to make sure the tube can migrate upward from the small bowel to the stomach or from the stomach to the esophagus. You'll want to check tube graduation marks, aspirating gastric residuals, and air auscultation, for starters. We can't do the x-ray confirmation, which is the gold standard, so it's imperative you listen to Allison and watch Cici closely. I remember you've had some hospital experience. Do you think you can handle this?"

"Yes, anything to keep Cici alive and at home."

"Now, there's one thing to consider. The bed must be at a 30–to 45-degree angle. Can you make the necessary adjustments before Allison arrives?"

"Yes, I'll do that. We can trust her, right?"

"Yes, definitely. There's a lot more she'll need to show you. She'll put in a catheter, for example. Just be a good student."

"Thank you for all your help. How much do I owe you?"

"Nothing for now. I'll pay the nurse and cover the supplies. We'll settle up later."

"How long will she linger in this state?"

"I don't know. It could be a few days. Then again, it could take weeks. Maybe months. The best we can do is take one day at a time."

Chapter 13

Currying Favor

EXCITEMENT STIRS THE AIR this morning. Madame Virginie is preparing for a new look. A special event is coming up that requires a fresh summery take on a New Orleans social season that involves operas, masked balls, dinner parties and charity events. She's eager to see what Marie Laveau has conjured up. Today is dress rehearsal.

The staff is bustling about, also anticipating Marie's arrival. Through them, she milks the underground gossip hotline to curry favors, conjure spells, and heal little ones. Marie is adept at creating potions purportedly granting eternal life and mind control, performing fertility rituals, and holding the key to transmutation, levitation, and necromancy. Daunting tasks!

Julie moves in and out of the room, checking on comings and goings. She returns from one jaunt, chuckling. "My sister is using powder for her face that's made from, um, young corn that's scraped and placed in water until the starch settles. She thinks it looks good. But it makes her look like an idiot."

Despite the bustle surrounding her arrival, Marie slips into the mansion with little fanfare. Zombi isn't with her. She stops at the stables on the way up, then the slave quarters, and finally the kitchen. She has "moles" to pay off and intel to gather. She feels the belly of a very pregnant servant and says authoritatively the baby is breach but should turn soon. She inquires about the baby daddy, who is, in this case, her husband. In these days, it's not uncommon for the man of the house to take liberties with the help. She asks another slave about his health. "Yeah, I got over that bad cough, thank you, Miz Marie."

Marie moves to Virginie's boudoir, with several decorative hair nets in tow. Confined styled hair is mostly worn by younger women, but Virginie considers herself young enough and Marie answers the call.

Hairnets, often called snoods, are typically made of fine material to match the wearer's natural hair color. Every so often, more elaborate versions are constructed of thin strips of velvet or chenille or decorated with beads. Marie pulls out a hairnet trimmed with ribbon ruchings designed to tightly fit the crown of the head.

Normally, social events peter out as summer wanes, but this year, in part because it's wartime, a herculean effort is underfoot to grease the social wheel. People need distractions from what's coming.

"Now, Madame Virginie, I have a few ideas for next week's ball," Marie says, enthusiastically. "If you don't like these hair nets, we can always part your hair in the center, roll or turn it up at the sides, and put flowers in it."

Virginie mulls the options, then demands, "Let's try them all!"

A seamstress – Sally Page, Julie whispers – appears from the back. As Marie hovers over Virginie's head, Sally focuses intently on embroidering silver onto a low neckline, double silk, triangular bodice. Its rich, magenta color was made popular by England's fashion queen, Harriet Sutherland-Leveson-Gower, the Duchess of Sutherland, also known as Queen Victoria's Mistress of the Robes.

It is said the Duchess started the Artistic Dress movement, which wouldn't reach America until 1861 or 1862. The dress is characterized by juliette sleeves, a slight train, the soft colors of vegetable dyes, and voluminous silk, velvet, and muslin fabrics. They were often worn without a corset or hoops. For now, having double bodices is practical; one is short sleeve, the other long sleeve. Virginie will complete the look with a square paisley shawl. Oppressive, steamy heat be damned.

"Not too bouffant," Virginie snaps her fingers at Sally, pointing to the nearby skirt being built. "It's not that special an occasion. But use plenty of lace, certainly for a fine collar."

Women's skirts at the time were the fullest ever. It easily took half a dozen yards of fabric and gauze lining to fully gather the bell-shaped skirt over cage crinolines, hoops, and starched petticoats. That's why some socialites, perhaps suffering economic woes, had dresses made from voluminous velvet curtains taken from upstairs windows toward the back of the house. But if the color wasn't purple or mauve or made with new-to-market brilliant pink aniline dyes, everybody knew.

"Good choice, Madame." Sally's right eye twitches as she nods. Marie peers at her sideways. These two professionals seem to peacefully coexist on Madame's team, but evidently no love is lost between them.

Marie holds out her feet while a cobbler dressed in all black tries on different shoes – pairs of black point-toe slippers, clunky black mules, and bootlettes dyed a complementary, darker pink.

"I like the dark magenta," Marie offers without being asked.

Virginie claps her hands with delight, kicking out her feet like a little girl. The cobbler moves out of the way to avoid being clobbered. "That's it, then. Pink shoes!" she shrieks.

Virginie wants to see glove possibilities, deciding between short pairs made of silk and lace or crocheted fingerless mittens. She chooses the latter, thinking it will provide some ventilation for a hot evening of hand kissing.

After vacillating between hairdo options, Virginie chooses a hairnet trimmed with light pink ribbon ruchings. She stands up and twirls through rose water Marie sprays in the air. Unlike many Creole women, Virginie has a particularly good figure, and makes just about any gown look spectacular. Dressing the difficult woman has its perks.

When the session is over, Virginie looks like she's ready to walk out the door to join high society. But it's all a facade. The staff is fine-tuning elements needed to make certain Madame lands on the society pages of The Picayune or in L'Abeille, a Creole newspaper.

Marie asks innocently, "What's Master Avegno wearing?"

"I don't keep up. Probably a ditto suit," Virginie answers with indifference. "He always looks fashionable."

The three-piece ditto suit was the menswear of the day. It consists of a loosely fitted sack coat, waistcoat and full trousers made of the same fabric. It emerged as a fad from England, as baggy loungewear made of wool. He won't need an overcoat in August, but a very tall stovepipe silken hat is required at all times.

Sally nods affirmatively. "He's wearing a dark suit. It'll work nicely with Madame's gown."

One might never know Virginie had filed for divorce the year before, citing cruelty and unusual punishment. She had gone to great lengths to cover at least one black eye. Divorce was an unthinkable move for a Creole woman, especially a Catholic one, and the filing quietly disappeared.

Perhaps Virginie wasn't given a choice in the proceedings because her husband worked the legal system. Or maybe she stopped it because she would lose custody of Mimi, who had discovered the 1860 papers in Virginie's boudoir and showed them to Julie. They pledged a vow of secrecy. Then they confided in me. Somehow, Marie already knew and enjoyed playing with Virginie's secret.

"He'll look quite handsome," Marie taunts.

"Yes, certainly," Virginie responds, jutting out her jaw.

Julie slides into the room and whispers something in Marie's ear while slipping her a crumpled note. Marie nods, slides the note discreetly into a side pocket, and with a fluid movement, returns to the task at hand.

"Marie, what is that?" Virginie asks.

"It's a note about another perfume you might like for your special night," Marie lies.

"I'm satisfied with rose water," Virginie says, curtly. She doesn't even ask about the nonexistent scent. The message, you see, regarded me. Waving her hands with a flourish, Virginie dismisses everyone.

If today's appointment had involved a haircut, Marie might've saved the clippings to burn, depending on Madame's behavior. Allegedly, if hair-combings are tossed away, birds may weave them into nests, causing a migraine to the person to whom the hair belongs. If the hair is burned, a voodoo practitioner can read the burning pattern as it relates to the hair owner's life. For example, a brightly burning blaze could mean the person's life will be long and content. But if it varies – doesn't catch fire or burns slowly – it could spell considerable illness and inescapable death.

# # #

Sitting at the foot of the bed in Julie's room, I struggle to stretch muscles without shooting pain in my legs. Determined to make progress, I stand with my feet wide apart and bend over until my head almost touches the floor when Julie and Marie walk in. My ass is their view. They do a double take and glance at each other.

"What are you doing?" Julie asks, as she briskly approaches to help me return to a "normal" posture.

"Just trying to stretch," I explain, knowing it must look unusual in the days before Jane Fonda fitness routines.

"Well, just sit down on this bed here, missy," Marie orders. I quickly comply. I'd used a bowl of water and a rough-edged rag to clean myself as best I could. At least the blood is cleaned up, tears wiped away; the urine and feces smell is almost gone.

Marie plants the back of her hand on my forehead. Satisfied I'm still fever-free, she relaxes.

"The worst is over. Now we need to get the rest of you well. But first, I must know ... why are you here?"

I clam up.

Something about the way she asks the question makes me realize she already knows the answer.

"Jules, give us a minute," Marie asks, without looking in her direction.

Julie obediently leaves the room. Marie draws a chair close to me and plops down, keeping her eyes fixed on mine the entire time. She draws inches to my face, her meaty breath falling hard on my neck. What has she been eating? I shudder to think.

"Now, what gives? You know I know you're not being straight with us. I know more than you can understand. And you know more than I can understand. We can work together, but I must know what I'm dealing with."

I'd been so wrapped up in misery, I hadn't thought it through. How much should I tell her? What should I keep to myself? How much of a danger does she pose? How much of an ally could she be? After all, she saved me from a miserable state. But then again, knowing human nature, she did it with a goal in mind. She doesn't strike me as a "goodness of the heart" kind of gal.

I turn the tables. "Why do you think I'm here?"

"So, you want to play it this way?

"I'd say you messed up your life. I'd say you wanted to end it. But just before death took your hand, you tumbled into a time portal.

You're wearing a cotton gown that I've never seen before, not from this period. The cotton, it's different ... woven loosely. You talk funny. You use words I've never heard. You know more than you're sharing, so it leads me to believe you've seen many things and are well read. You have scars all over your body, but they look neat and tidy. The cuts weren't done with a crude knife. Your hair has fake color; it's more sophisticated coloring than what I use.

"So, tell me when you're from."

I swallow hard.

Marie was uncomfortably spot-on with her assessment. Would it behoove me to give her dates?

"What time do you think I'm from?"

Marie taps her cheek with a gnarly finger, glittering with an early version of black nail polish she didn't have on the day before. What had she dipped her nails in?

"Hard to say. I don't know much about the future, though some," she says, ominously. "I know about the Spanish influenza deaths that occur sometime next century. But something tells me you're past that."

It's fascinating hearing her line of thought. I wonder if I should give her a hint.

"You're on the right track," I say, encouragingly.

"I know there are a couple of world wars, with birds in the sky dropping death, but you seem to be past those, too."

"True," I admit. How does she know about World Wars I and II?

"I can't guess past that." With that statement, Marie settles back into the rocking chair and impatiently awaits an answer.

"It's a long time from now," I admit. "It's in the 21st century."

Marie maintains a poker face. She doesn't have the answer she wants.

"Ok, 2019," I say, sighing nervously.

Marie looks off in the distance as she calculates her stance.

"We can work with that."

Chapter 14

Puppet Master

JULIE SLIPS INTO THE ROOM and alerts Marie Laveau a servant has taken ill.

"It's Jeremiah," explains Julie. "He's the one with a wife and two sons. He should be worth checking on."

Julie knows Marie's motives. It's better to help someone beholden to others than to spend time healing a solitary person with no familial ties.

"Before I go ... about getting Cici healed, here's what we're going to do," says Marie, turning to Julie. "We'll have a basic gris gris ceremony. I'll bring snakeskin. You'll need to bring three copper pennies, rose petals and lavender flowers, and wrap it all in a chamois cloth and place it in a leather bag. Maybe flannel. Sally should be able to help you without asking questions. Can you handle the rest?"

"Yes, of course."

"What's that for?" I ask. Marie looks irritated by the question.

"We're going to call on Papa Labat to rid you of this pain. Not just your physical aches, but also to mend a broken heart and soul. We're going to say a chant while we're touching the gris gris to the top of your head, your heart and then you're going to kiss the bag."

Marie throws back her head for dramatic effect and gives us a preview of the chanting. It amazes me how her turban stays put.

"Papa Labat, yay, yay yay Papa Labat, yay yay, yay, Papa Labat, yay yay yay Papa Labat, open the door and let the spirits through. Bless and empower this bag for your faithful servant. Bring her all good things in this life and in the life to come in God's name. Ashe', ashe', ashe'!"

I was surprised to hear God's name mentioned, but voodoo is a sister to Catholicism, giving Marie a complex take on good and evil.

Marie confers with Julie about me also needing good luck. "We'll mix oils – cinnamon and vanilla – with wintergreen and water to scrub the floor under the bed," Marie decides.

Before Marie leaves the room, she tells me: "This isn't over yet. We're going to talk. And next time, I want every little detail."

With a swish of her skirts, Marie departs.

Julie takes Marie's place in the chair and asks if I'm alright.

"Just a bit startled by her questions," I admit. "I trust you. But I get a funny feeling about Marie. I know some things about her, but there are many blanks."

Julie pauses. When the silence becomes uncomfortable, I ask her opinion.

"Cici, I'm going to tell you some important details about Marie's life," she says. "I want you to keep it to yourself. I see the predicament you're in, and I want to help you survive whatever trap you've fallen into. I'll share two important points: one, Marie is dangerous, and you want to keep her close. Two, she can help you in ways you cannot imagine. She may even be able to reunite you with your husband. And when the time is right, ask about the Pool of Souls. Now she'll want something from you in return. Your job is to feed her enough information to gain her trust, but not enough to give her all the power. I can help with that. Do you want me to?"

I nod eagerly.

"Ok, what do you know about Marie? I'll fill in the blanks."

Not long ago, I'd researched Marie Laveau's life for a magazine project. But I yearned to fill in the blanks. Here's what I knew:

Marie Laveau's great-grandmother, Marguerite, lived in Senegal, West Africa. Slave traders sold her as a child to Europeans and stuck her on a slave ship to America, where she and her two-year-old daughter, Catherine, Marie's grandmother, became property of a white Creole, Henry Roche. He allegedly fathered several children of Catherine's, including Marguerite Darcantrel, Marie's mother. Catherine was only 13 when Marguerite was born; Marguerite was the same age when Marie was born. Charles Laveau, a wealthy, mulatto Creole and possibly the son of the surveyor general of Spanish Louisiana, fathered her.

Born September 10, 1801, Marie, the first free Creole in her family, was six days old when her parents presented her in the sanctuary of Saint Louis Cathedral, where Father Pere Antoine baptized her into the Catholic faith. Her godmother was her grandmother, Catherine. Her godfather was a Spaniard, Jose Joaquin Velasquez, a true Vito Corleone in his own right.

The famed Saint Louis Cathedral and Father Antoine played another major role in Marie's life, when, at the age of 18, on August 4, 1819, she married Jacque (Santiago) Paris, a carpenter and another free person of color. They lived on Rue Dauphine between Rues Dumaine and Saint Philip. Slight hitch: she purportedly had a child, Felicite, two years earlier that might have died around the age of seven.

Speculation swirled the marriage soured when her husband abandoned her, perhaps returning to San Domingue, Haiti, or joining the

Merchant Marines. Some say he was swept overboard. But the truer story may be that he died at the hands of Marie, who became known as the "Widow Paris." One possibility: he's buried in the victory herb garden in the back of the Ursuline Convent, where Marie spends time on her knees tending plants, plucking herbs, and praying.

When she was 31, Marie joined a common-law marriage with Louis Christophe Dominique Duminy de Glapion, a wealthy white New Orleanian who served under Andrew Jackson in the Battle of 1815. Surprising fact: the couple owned slaves! In both marriages, Marie had at least seven children, some say up to 15. Three children died in infancy; only two survived to adulthood, including Marie Philomene Glapion, basically a clone of her mother who became the infamous Marie II, and embraced an even darker nature of voodoo.

Julie taps my arm to bring me out of my trance. "Let's start at the beginning. How much do you know about Marie Laveau, her upbringing and such?"

I tell her what I learned about Marie Laveau's childhood, heritage, and marriages, and that she had been a protégé of the famous Voodooist Dr. John.

"Am I right so far?"

"You're telling me things I didn't know. Carry on."

"Here are some of the stranger things I heard about Marie Laveau," I start. "That she sold her soul to Papa Legba, the spiritual gatekeeper between worlds. And that she must gift him a yearly sacrifice in the form of the soul of an innocent child."

"Well, that might be a bit much," Julie ponders the statement.

"Then there's the one about the woman with a diseased leg who sought Marie's medical help. Marie boiled up a batch of snakes, made a powder, and rubbed it all over the woman's leg. Onlookers insist they saw a snake crawling under her skin from her foot to her stomach. Then, she began vomiting snails. A sore popped open on her leg and maggots fell to the floor. When she died, nobody wanted to embalm her because they swore a frog was croakin' in her throat. And Cajuns hate frogs. Could that be true?"

Marie is all about magical prowess – much of it good, Julie corrects me.

"She's tended those with yellow fever, conjured up spells and medicinal herbs to help people, like you," she reminds me. "She's healed the sick from the brink of death. She's spent time 'freeing' men from the gallows of death row at Pariah Prison.

"But if you cross her people, she's unforgiving. For example, the police routinely harass Marie, and that's not good for them."

The legend of snake boiling might not be too far-fetched. Marie lives at 152 Rue Saint Ann, more recently known as 1020 Rue Saint Ann, where I hear she keeps crates full of snakes covered by tightly woven wire in the back yard garden. I ask Julie if it's true.

"I don't know, but it's possible."

Despite folklore of gaining the cottage on Rue Saint Ann in nefarious ways, it was her childhood home, purchased by her grandmother, Catherine.

Legend has it that one of Marie's greatest coups involved getting an affluent family's son off rape charges. But some say the young lady's family was affluent while the son's parents were not. Whichever the case, when the trial began, it seemed a cinch for the prosecution to win, which would result in death by hanging. But reports share that, during the trial, she spent early-morning hours on her knees, praying at the foot of the Virgin Mary in the Saint Louis Cathedral, with a trio of Guinea peppers in her mouth, which she then deposited under the judge's chair. Another account tells she placed three gris gris bags around the courtroom before the trial. When the case was dismissed, some wondered if the peppers or gris gris bags had anything to do with it. Chances are, Marie had the goods on the judge.

"Isn't that crazy?"

"It's possible," Julie says, then waits for me to continue the modern-day musings of Marie Laveau.

It seems premature to share how many hawkers make money off Marie. Ground zero for tackiness seems to be 739 Bourbon, home of the Marie Laveau House of Voodoo – a shrine, gift store, museum, and cash cow. How can I tell Julie a cast of characters suck twenties from gullible tourists through readings of palms and tarot cards in her honor? Some readers get more specific, requesting Vedic palmistry, a more introspective, inclusive reading. The House also sells overpriced, spindly candles of every color to burn for various purposes. White is for peace; red for victory; pink for love; lavender to cause harm; blue for success and protection; and black for evil.

The truer ground zero for the Laveau clan might be Cornrow City, which Marie (and Marie II) seems to use as a modern-day call center. It's a hairdressing salon in the 9th ward that somehow survived the ravaging aftermath of Hurricane Katrina in 2005. Or Congo Square, now known as Louis Armstrong Park, where many mysterious gatherings are held.

I was lost in my thoughts when Julie asks, rather tentatively, "what else?"

"I've heard Marie runs New Orleans," I continue. "She knows secrets of many people, particularly the city's most well-bred. It's their fault, really, for confiding in Marie while she does their hair. They blab without thinking. If it isn't in her best interest to see a politician elected, or a proposed law move forward, she pulls strings to achieve a favorable result."

"You're on the right track," Julie confirms. "Now I'll tell you interesting bits.

"The first thing to know about Marie is her absolute power climaxes every Saint John's Eve. It occurs around summer solstice every year, on June 23, and ends at dawn the following day."

Saint John's Eve is the most sacred holiday in the voodoo faith, an extended all-night ritual that attracts hundreds of followers. It's an Afro-Caribbean holy day that involves nude dancing, animal sacrifice, bonfires on the levy, and Marie's much talked-about orgies along Bayou Saint John.

"On that day, they do ceremonial voodoo baptisms, which essentially means washing heads," Julie explains. "Everyone wears white, sometimes head to toe, while others may only have a kerchief. White marks them."

The Calinda, she describes, is a Louisiana swamp voodoo dance that gains strength and power until it's a highly lascivious performance as Damballa is summoned. Lewd acts draw out Damballa, whose dreads are squirming snakes, usually when the bonfire is white-hot.

"But wasn't the dance considered so indecent, it was outlawed years ago?"

"Yes, about 20 years ago, I believe," Julie nods. "But that didn't stop anyone. I'll tell you more about it later, but right now, what do you want to know about?"

I'd heard about the LaLaurie family and the savage secrets playing out behind the moneyed facade of Aubusson carpets, horsehair sofas, Victorian lamps, and heavy mahogany furnishings inlaid with maple and ebony veneer. And I'd wondered if Marie had anything to do with the demise of the LaLaurie mansion, the French Quarter's modern-day most famous haunted house.

"Yes, she did, but nobody will say anything about it. If you mention any connection, people look at you funny.

"Now, this is just hearsay. I wasn't around at the time. It was many years back. Madame Delphine LaLaurie was a socialite that everyone put up with because of her wealth. She seemed odd, and loved good gossip, but nothing anyone could point to, until a 12-year-old slave girl jumped to her death from the third-floor balcony of the LaLaurie mansion. Madame LaLaurie was caught trying to bury the girl's body in an old courtyard well. When they uncovered the girl, she had whip markings on her back. I guess the poor thing couldn't take it anymore."

"Didn't the police do anything?"

"Ha! You mean the Not Our Problem, Darling gang? Madame LaLaurie got a slap on the wrist. She had to pay some $300 fine for slave abuse. They sold her slaves at public auction. But her friends bought them back and she ended up with them anyway."

In those days, slaves were paraded through the alley at Exchange Place on their way to auction blocks that frequently took place in the rotunda of the Saint Louis Hotel, built in 1838 at the corner of Rues Saint Louis and Chartres, now known as Omni Royal Orleans. Most slaves had arrived in America via high-walled slave pens on ships. Smaller auctions were held on the decks of ships moored along the Mississippi River.

"And the torture continued?"

"Nobody knew about the experiments at the time. It wasn't until a house cook deliberately started a fire in 1834 that brought firemen to the house. And then everything quickly unraveled.

"On the third floor, they found slaves chained to the walls. Naked male slaves had their eyes gouged out, lips sewn together, and ears hanging by shreds of flesh ... fingernails had been pulled out by their roots."

Julie grimaces while recalling the gruesome practices.

"Some had joints skinned and festering. Others had holes in their, um, bottoms, where flesh had been carved up. Some slaves had intestines pulled out and knotted around their waists. Some have gone so far as to say Madame LaLaurie used intestines as balcony garland during Mardi Gras, but I think that's a bit much. One woman had her arms amputated and skinned to resemble a caterpillar. Another had broken limbs reset to look like a crab. And the worst: some slaves' heads had been cracked open with a rod. Someone had been stirring their brains! But those were the living dead. Madame LaLaurie is said to have killed more than 70 slaves."

Julie told how the entire community stormed the house.

"While firemen were busy discovering this human suffering, some say Madame LaLaurie and her husband, Dr. Lou, escaped by carriage. They crossed Saint John's Bayou in a schooner to Saint Tammany Parish to settle along the North Shore. Another rumor is they fled to Paris. Either way, nobody heard from them again."

"Where does Marie come in?"

"Madame LaLaurie had publicly humiliated Marie when she was quite young and new to hairdressing. Apparently, Madame LaLaurie didn't like the style Marie did for her and she carried on to anyone who would listen. Marie never forgot it. Well, thanks to Marie, some say, everybody became convinced that Madame LaLaurie was behind the experiments and her reputation was ruined. All the while, her surgeon husband was toiling away in his mad scientist lab."

The doctor connection reminded me of the eccentric pharmacist who buried customers in his 1823 Creole townhouse. Dr. "Death" Dupas was a protégé of the first licensed pharmacist in the United States, Louis J. Dufilho, Jr., and bought the pharmacy from him. Dressed alternately in a lab coat or proper brown suit, and seemingly full of medical knowledge, the community trusted him. After all, a reputable doctor kept an office and optical shop on the second floor.

However, dead bodies won't be found underneath herbs and flowers, the floorboards, and other cubbyholes until 1867. Right now, he's experimenting.

"What's the deal with the local pharmacist?" I dummy up. "I don't know much about him. I hardly ever go there. He acts weird but he dresses nice. Marie practically lives there," Julie says, with a quizzical look. "She buys and sells herbs and potions and seems to be quite cozy with him."

In fact, he sold pills and powders of every concoction, horrifically oversized hypodermic needs, therapeutic bloodletting tools, and leeches. He prepared medicines to battle dysentery, malaria, yellow fever, and other epidemics and maladies. He allegedly concocted an early version of the trademarked One Night Cough Syrup, containing alcohol, cannabis, chloroform and morphine.

"Do you remember hearing Marie say anything about Dr. Dupas?"

"They had a falling out once or twice, I believe," Julie says, tapping her chin. "But Marie seems to have gotten over it."

Against my better judgment, I tell Julie what I'd learned about the pharmacist.

Julie clasps her hand over her mouth, horrified at the thought of people being cavalierly murdered without consequence for years. "Should we do something? Don't we have an obligation?" She catches herself and shakes her head.

"Based on everything I've heard about it, Marie put a curse of syphilis on the pharmacist, who slowly turns mad," I explain. "This is probably happening now. When he dies in six years, police will find bodies of missing patients buried all over the place. He tried some appalling medical experiments on pregnant slaves. When questioned about certain disappearances before he went mad, he insisted the missing people returned to France."

"Oh, no," Julie moans. "This is terrible. But it all makes sense!"

"I heard that, after the syphilis started, customers would catch him throwing books against the wall or absentmindedly reorganizing displays."

We vow to keep details of the pharmacist mum. For now.

Julie disappears to get us sweet tea, while I absorb this new information. When she returns, I ask if Marie is a lady of the night.

"You mean, a whore?" Julie laughs, with a snort.

"No, she wouldn't lower herself to those standards. She has prostitutes working for her! You need to stay away from those places, especially Gallatin Street," Julie warns.

Located where the French Market stands today, Gallatin Street in the early 1860s is a prostitution district lined with ramshackle houses slapped together by unstable wooden planks. Brothel runners Mary Jane "Bricktop" Jackson and Bridget Fury, will become well-known for allegedly bludgeoning nonpaying and unruly customers with an axe. The Live Oak gang is known for even more violent crimes. Before the end of the decade, the prostitution district will be pushed farther into Vieux Carre.

I venture further with another story. "I also heard about a bar just outside the Quarter where its owners were cursed. I believe four owners died in succession within a decade. Did Marie have anything to do with that?"

"Probably. She has a way of pulling strings from both ends."

I asked about the Ursuline Convent. What did Marie have to do with its haunting? Built in 1752 as the oldest surviving example of America's French Colonial era, it protects the treasure of the Archdiocesan archives. From the Chartres Street Gatehouse entrance, a magnificently manicured formal garden leads to the main building and a vestibule that houses an exquisite, original hand-crafted cypress staircase. Beyond that is a peaceful walled courtyard designed for prayer and contemplation.

Over centuries, the main lodge – brimming with oil paintings, statues, and bronze busts of Catholic higher-ups – has served as a convent, orphanage, military hospital, and residence hall for local bishops.

The impressive landmark has a dark side. When young French girls began arriving at the convent in the late 1700s, they were called filles a la cassette, or "casket girls," because their belongings arrived in a casket the nuns stored on the third floor.

"Rumors flew that casket girls smuggled vampires who rested in those caskets," Julie says, folding her hands into a praying position and lowering her voice. "In fact, word has it the nuns bolted and permanently shut the third-floor shutters, so the vampires couldn't escape."

Eerily, Ursuline nuns are buried under the floorboards of the convent's music room.

"Back in 1978, curious reporters tried to gain access to the convent's third floor, but ended up as unsolved murders," I share. "The two climbed over the Ursuline Convent wall and set up a covert reconnaissance base with recording devices. The next day, their equipment was found strewn across the lawn and their dead bodies were found on the porch steps."

Julie's eyes widen. "Now I'm curious. I want to go over there and see what's happening. But not at the risk of foul play."

I ask Julie if Marie had anything to do with the tragedy of the stunning Gardette-LePretre House at 716 Rue Dauphine. A rich sultan, the younger brother of Turkish king Prince Suleyman, met a harsh, untimely death, along with his entourage harem of roughly 48 girls and women, plus the sultan's loyal eunuch. For too long, neighbors had put up with the smell of heavy incense, loud music, and extravagant absinthe and opium parties.

Some say the sultan arrived in New Orleans with money and jewels stolen from his brother, who might have ordered a small army of professional assassins to handle the mass execution. But I'm getting ahead of myself again. One morning, a neighbor noticed streams of blood coming from the house. Officers found all occupants dead – dismembered in the house with the sultan buried alive in the backyard. It's New Orleans' second-most haunted palace.

"No, I don't think so," Julie guesses. "Believe it or not, Marie is not that cruel. Deep in her heart, she's a kind soul. Her best attribute is probably that she's fair."

Like Hannibal Lector's character, I thought, where only the mean-spirited or untalented are eliminated.

Before we could compare more Marie notes, Mimi comes running into the room, closing the door quickly behind her, and stopping to catch her breath.

"Tante Julie, Tante Julie, come quick!"

"What is it, child?"

"Ollie needs us!" Mimi grabs Julie's hand and they rush downstairs, shoes clattering on the stairs.

Finding myself alone is happening more frequently. But it's good for me to figure things out as quickly as possible to survive this crazy twist of fate.

Chapter 15

Another Ally

A SURPRISING PARTNER arrives in the form of Sally Page. She has a similar connection in an exceedingly small way to the same pipeline as Marie Laveau. According to Julie, Marie knows a secret about Sally that insures she will never be any trouble.

"Whatever it is, it's bad," Julie says, with a frown.

Sally became an ally when she was overbooked with tailoring duties. Learning that I was a seamstress well versed in a few valuable techniques, and that I needed money but more importantly than that, to remain low-key and have some place in society, she contracted me to draw sketches, do fittings, sew hems, some embroidery, and assist with fabric selection.

The 1860s elaborate antebellum gowns are too much as a whole; bits and pieces suit me well. I became more useful after Sally taught me how to tack narrow vertical pleats in the back of mantua bodices so they would fit the wearer like a second skin. The secret: sewing tiny, interlocking stitches that can withstand the tension across the figure and avoid unattractive wrinkling. She also showed me how to starch petticoats with sugar water, so the skirt fans out almost parallel to the floor.

I'm in awe of Sally's sewing machine, a new-fangled device for the time. It's protected by a solid redwood case, silver plated and embellished with enamel and inlaid pearl. It had been gifted to her from Confederate upper-crust clients who read the writing on the wall concerning the direction of the Civil War. It behooved them to be rid of certain valuables.

Sally also tutored me in the art of skirt sewing – how to use longer, looser stitches so seams don't crumple and spoil the lines of the gown. Later, I made simple, long-sleeved dresses with high necklines and collars with little adornment. Hoping I would return to Parker and modern-day New Orleans soon, I didn't bother to learn more highly skilled sewing techniques.

As I converse with Sally, I cannot help but wonder her secret. What is so damning that Marie could hold it over her head indefinitely. Did she have a child out of wedlock, sired by a Creole master, perhaps? Was she the product of the same? Those situations are not uncommon. I'd soon learn her surprise was more ruinous than anything I might have considered.

Julie, a master networker in her own right, brought us together. After the dress-up session with Marie and Virginie, Julie had discreetly brought Sally to her bedroom, introduced us, and explained the situation. Sort of.

"Cici is visiting until she gets well," Julie says. "She had a minor illness that's clearing up nicely. Nothing anybody can catch. Since she's worked as a seamstress, I thought she might help you out."

"I'm rusty," I confess.

"That's ok," Sally remarks. "If you know the basics, you're teachable. And I could use the help."

"I'd love to," I reply, eyeing possibilities beyond the obvious. One perk: it would also allow me to accompany Sally to socialites' boudoirs. Information is gold.

"Then it's settled," Sally responds, with a smile.

Sally's father, James Page, arrived in New Orleans as a slave via the Schooner Thomas Hunter on Nov. 11, 1835. His height was a mere 5'1". Sally is a few inches taller, with a slight built, a flawless coffee-cream complexion and chocolate almond-shaped eyes. Her hair is combed over her head and fashionably fastened in a tight low bun. She's polite, appreciative, and soft-spoken.

Very streetwise, Sally smartly dresses in shades that allow her to morph effortlessly into the background. The only color that stands out is the 120-inch faded yellow tape measure that hangs around her neck like jewelry. But she speaks with an almost tenor voice that appears out of place for a delicate lady. Perhaps that's why she doesn't speak much, especially around Marie? Hmm.

Sally motions to the dress parts in hand, her right eye twitching again at the mention of Virginie's name. "Madame needs the magenta gown within 10 days. Julie needs a simpler gown. Maybe you can do some sketches for her and let me know quickly what she settles on. That is, if she's going to the ball."

Julie nods affirmatively.

"What about Mimi?" I ask, ignorantly. "What will she wear?"

"Mimi doesn't attend social events yet," she gently explains. "When she's a few years older, she'll wear a junior gown."

I blush with embarrassment. Why can I not keep my mouth shut?

Chapter 16

Pecking Order

TO UNDERSTAND 1861 NEW ORLEANS, it's important to know about Creole culture, an aristocratic and feudal organization based on slavery, and the Avegnos' secure place in society.

Filippe Guiseppe Avegno, whose Creole family made their vast fortune building ships in Italy and transporting crops such as bat guano fertilizer, immigrated from Camogli in 1823. He married Catherine Genois in a beneficial union; she was a Louisiana Creole.

Their son, Anatole Placide Avegno, was born July 3, 1835, in Orleans Parish. He made a good match with Virginie Ternant, who was 18 when they met at a Saint Louis Hotel masked ball.

On the surface, Anatole was a successful attorney with a busy law practice on Camp

Street, and a stand-up citizen who had helped resurrect Mardi Gras parades just three years earlier. He built the tallest residential structure in New Orleans at 927 Rue Toulouse and enjoyed a stratospheric rise in social standing due to his Creole nature.

Interestingly and without merit, Creoles like the Avegnos believe themselves superior. Like many Creoles, Anatole works in a profession in which he never gets his hands dirty, rarely needing to remove his coat. He is always impeccably dressed, appearing in public with coat, cravat and gloves, no matter the weather.

Like most Creoles, Anatole appears to be a warm, affectionate, polite, and loyal man. Even though he runs the household with an iron fist, he is charitable, steadfast, and kind-hearted. That said, if a Creole family member marries someone with mixed-race blood, it calls for total familial ostracism. You see, only pure-bred white people are considered true Creoles.

Julie schooled me on the finicky bunch, warning me they despise Americans, whom they eye suspiciously and generally consider wicked.

I need to continue to fly under the radar to avoid suspicion. No faux pas accepted.

Here's an interesting, yet confusing reality during antebellum times: Concerning social manners, Creoles speak French almost exclusively. If a Spanish-speaking Creole marries into a French Creole family, the couple transitions to only speaking French. Americans refuse to learn French for Creoles' sake. Once, the feud between the Creoles and the rest of New Orleans grew so contemptuous that only a New Orleans boulevard divided their worlds. Who knew Canal Street was neutral ground?

"*Pal franse pa di lespri pou sa,*" Julie recants. "That's a Haitian Creole saying that means 'speaking French doesn't mean you're smart.'"

We both have a good laugh.

"Here's the confusing part," I remark. "I know very little French. Why is English spoken in the household?"

"You're fine. Sally doesn't speak much French. Marie rarely does. The Avegnos only resort to speaking French when they're talking about something confidential or they're out in society."

Oddly, narcissistic tendencies fail most Creole women. With little desire to curb their food intake, many are obese, perhaps also from having a litter of children. A proper Creole wife is a marvelous madame of the house, making sure the house is spotless and the meals are splendid.

Virginie Avegno easily rose to the task.

I've never enjoyed tastier food and good wine than in the Avegno household. Most meals start with crab gumbo, include a rich oyster stew, and all main courses include poultry, beef, and fish from French and Spanish recipes. On special occasions, a roasted, milk-fed suckling pig is the centerpiece. Red beans seasoned with ham or salt pork is a staple. As is chicory coffee, which has a hint of chocolate. Lagniappe comes in the form of cakes, candies, and pies for the family and servants. Typically, at least two dessert choices accompany every dinner meal.

Pralines are special treats, a sweet French confection made simply of fresh milk, cream, butter, sugar, and jumbo pecans.

Creoles define their own brand of contradiction. When they're not being gracious hosts, with etiquette refinement, Creole women often sit in rocking chairs smack dab in the middle of a sidewalk, forcing pedestrians to walk around them, and whispering about them as they pass. This is as true in 2019 as 1861. Creoles' sense of grandiosity and reputation as gossip mongers is legendary.

Yet "proper" social circling is the Creole wife's primary asset. She knows how to dance, play the piano, carry on a brilliant conversation, and wrest her family to church. When boys are old enough, they're typically sent to Paris for a French education, while girls are dispatched to local convents, such as the Ursuline Convent, led by French nuns.

"There are all sorts of rules for remarrying. If my sister dies, I'd probably be expected to marry her husband, to keep the children in the family," Julie rolls her eyes. "But if the husband dies, Creole women are draped in black and stay in mourning for years and aren't expected to remarry. Then again, if a cat dies in the household, the family wears black for mourning."

"A cat? Really?" I shake my head in disbelief.

"That's right," Julie snickers. "Creoles are very superstitious. Mimi is not too many years from following a time-tested ritual."

When she's a young teen with an eye toward marriage, for example, Mimi will take a stance by her bed on the first Friday of every month and say, "Today ... I place my foot on the footboard and I pray to the great Saint Nicholas to help me meet the one I am to marry." Then, she'll jump into bed without touching the floor, sleep on her right side, hand over her heart, Julie explains.

"She can't laugh. She can't talk. She can't move or the spell will be broken," Julie emphasizes.

Another Creole delusion: If you sleep with moonlight on your face, you'll go crazy.

"That's one of the many things they said about me," Julie laughs.

Creoles have their own take on holidays. On a Saint's day, special cakes are consumed. No King cake, but rather a spongey sort of dessert, typically with a rose stuck in the middle.

Christmas is more about attending Midnight Mass, hot eggnog, and the proper amount of whiskey than having presents strewn under a tree. Better presents are given on New Year's Day. But it's a rather formal event.

"On New Year's morning, gifts are opened practically at the crack of dawn," explains Julie. "But not before children present their parents with a very precise gift. For example, they'll give them a carefully prepared sheet of pink paper, brimming with plump cherubs ringing silvery tinsel bells, and containing a certain biblical verse."

Holy Week is a year-high event for Creoles, who, on Good Friday, visit nine churches on foot and in silence in exchange for good luck.

"Seems this lifestyle doesn't leave much room for a rebel," I observe.

"That's true. I suppose I'm a rebel. And even though I'm not out of the family entirely, I'm somewhat of an outcast."

In other words, one learns to skirt the hoodoo-isms.

Perhaps the most impressive Creole attribute is their loyalty to state and country.

On Sept. 13, 1861, Avegno will leave his law practice to enlist in the Confederate States of America military. Along with his brother, Jean-Bernard Avegno, they will recruit an entire Governor Guards' Battalion called "Avegno Zouaves." He'll command the 13th Louisiana Infantry Regiment that includes Chinese, French, Irish, Italian, Mexican and Spanish soldiers among six companies.

On the second day of the 1862 Battle of Shiloh, Anatole will be shot in the left leg that will require medical attention outside their scarce resources. The battalion's dress uniform may unwittingly attract the enemy, a dark blue uniform with gold braids and shapeless silk trousers topped with a cardinal red cap that will bob with every movement. He'll be sent home by train to recover, but Anatole will die nearly two weeks later, on April 7, 1862, at Camp Moore in Amite, Louisiana, an hour after his leg is amputated above the knee. At the funeral, Virginie will wail histrionically, though in private, secretly admit relief. He will be buried in Saint Louis Cemetery No. 2.

I reveal none of this to Julie, who tires of the conversation and heads into her art studio while I mull the intricacies of these fascinating folks.

Chapter 17

The Manse

YEARS BEFORE TRAGEDY roiled our lives, Parker and I discovered the Madame X mansion at 927 Rue Toulouse, named after the socialite who grew up there and became famous for her portrait. The leasing sign guaranteed "no ghosts!" When did unhaunted become an amenity? We were intrigued to learn Napoleonic law defines "haunted" as "psychologically impacted."

We leased Apartment No. 5, sight unseen. Its unique character charmed us —red brick-plastered walls, diffused lighting, 14-foot ceilings, and crisscross transoms over tall, lean windows. French doors led to a palm-treed, cobblestone courtyard.

We noticed a problem right away. The property listing advertised 800 square feet, but the two-room flat was about half that size.

Pictures from the listing were of the apartment above. By comparison, our place had much less character. What's the deal with false advertising? We'd soon learn the French Quarter has its own rules, and only a fool would waste time fighting it. Nevertheless, I never knew two people could share such a tiny space.

Unsatisfying details aside, the mansion's storied anteroom charmed us. The door to No. 5 links directly to it, where a reproduction of enigmatic John Singer Sargent's controversial *Madame X* portrait is prominently displayed. A dazzlingly brilliant high-ceiling chandelier, framed by an elaborately carved ceiling medallion, illuminates the massive artwork. Billowy floor-length curtains heighten the space.

The original oil-on-canvas features a now-adult, voluptuous Mimi, a striking French Creole woman turned Paris's "it" girl, in a stunning black velvet dress with black gloves. Instead of the portrait being commissioned, Sargent had heavily pursued his subject. With her green eyes, porcelain face exotically made up, dominant nose, burnished copper hair twisted into a long roll at the back of her neck, rouged ears, arched eyebrows, and willowy body, she was a stellar model. He vowed to capture it in oils.

Mimi/Madame X shared in a letter: "Sargent begged me to sit for him. He stalked me like a hunter does a deer, staring at me at parties and getting his friends to pester me – 'Please, Madame Gatreau, let John pay homage to your great beauty.'"

This reproduction, sheltered under handsomely curved cypress stairs, shows two jeweled ballgown straps on pearly-white sculpted shoulders. But in the original, a lazily fallen shoulder strap spurred a surprising stream of profanity from sanctimonious gawkers when the canvas was unveiled at the Paris Salon in April 1884. Moral outrage nearly ruined the artist in a Victorian metropolis satiated with elicit liaisons. Terrible reviews became the socialite's worst nightmare. Her mother was said to have cried, *"Ma fille est perdue!"* translated to "my daughter is lost!" at the freshly unveiled painting. Madame X, who had so carefully crafted her elevated place in society, became an overnight recluse.

When we initially moved into the building, neighbors asked if we knew about Madame X. In the same breath, they frequently mentioned Marie Laveau. Forget politicians and celebrities. Did we know Marie was the underground ruler of New Orleans in her heyday? But mostly, they talked about the historical significance of 927 Rue Toulouse.

Anatole Avegno built the 8,500-square-foot compound near the height of antebellum splendor. He made sure the clay red plaster mansion with deep green shutters measured taller than any other structure in New Orleans.

Modern day, the mansion houses seven apartments, all accessible beyond a reinforced gate via an arched cobblestone carriageway. On the left of the anteroom, with black-and-white harlequin flooring, is Apartment No. 1, which once housed a storefront. It was converted into a 650-square-foot, one-bedroom apartment in which no one sleeps comfortably. Rows of glass windows provide little buffer from excessive street noise.

On the second of four floors is Apartment No. 2, the mansion's grand residence. Its glistening wood flooring and cream-colored plastered walls represent the ideal backdrop for a magnificent drawing room with a fireplace, two bedrooms, each with fireplaces and separated by pocket doors. It features a very narrow balcony with the initials "PP" (ironically, not "AA" for Anatole Avegno) set in the railing, and the tiniest kitchen imaginable.

No. 3 takes up the third floor with two bedrooms. It might well be where Anatole slept. Like many couples of the day, the husband and wife had separate boudoirs.

No. 4 is the penthouse, an overpriced, stifling space with a training pole for stripteasers. No. 5 is our cubbyhole, otherwise home to the horse stable. No. 6 is a two-level apartment of four equally spaced rooms that became Julie's home. No. 7 is another narrow apartment, where the 1861 kitchen was housed.

In this sumptuous house, enjoying the lifestyle to which they are accustomed, it's hard to believe that, in private, Anatole terrorizes Virginie. Once, I was coming home from a sewing assignment when Virginie clambered down the stairs, two steps at a time, trying to get away from Anatole. She had a black eye and bruises on her upper arms from being held too tightly. She stumbled on the last step and fell in a heap onto the marbled floor, her skirts billowing and exposing her derriere. When I tried to help her up, she defiantly turned away, eyes drenched in tears as she rushed to hide in a cubby under the stairs. Instead of a look of terror, she exuded pure hatred. She spoke to me with chilly disdain: "Get out of my way!" The episode unsettled me, and I feared I would soon be homeless.

Chapter 18

Battle of Wits

TODAY IS MY COMING OUT PARTY, of sorts. My tattered nightgown will be set aside for washing, if salvageable, and Sally is bringing over a couple of dresses appropriate for me to wear in the daytime. They belonged to out-of-town clients who, Sally explains with slight amusement, outgrew their clothing. They're supposed to be loose and won't require much alteration.

Marie Laveau will be coming over later today to check on me and to glean more information. She wants to negotiate. Julie and I have outlined a plan. I'll tell her just enough to remain interesting. I simply must return to Parker.

Thunderstorms roil in the distance. It's hurricane season and I missed a nasty one by about a week. In early August, winds clocked more than 150 miles per hour. Nothing flooded permanently and damage was minimal, though Julie said the skies cried for days and rats ran amok in the streets. Everything was almost back to normal when I arrived.

I happen to know a third hurricane of 1861 will take place October 2 and cause a storm surge to destroy lakefront villages and flood areas north of the Quarter. As usual, the Quarter will be spared. That nugget alone might curry favor with Marie. It's eerie to think I may have subconsciously been preparing for this adventure with my research.

Sally arrives with dresses and sewing projects. "I'll need you to come with me after you get ready. We're going to Madame's mother's place on Burgundy. She needs something for the big event, and honestly, she makes Virginie look reasonable."

She hands me the two-piece dress to put on. I start to slip the top half over my head when Sally and Julie burst out laughing.

"You've got a long way to go before the dress actually goes on," Julie says gently.

I was unprepared for all the fuss. First, a chemise goes on, then stockings. Second, foundation garments -- a corset and drawers. A blouse and skirt hoops come next. Finally, the dress. This one is a cream-colored two-piece with oversized, loosely gathered bishop sleeves for ventilation. Because it was made with a lighter weight cotton, it's called a "sheer dress." Its' definitely not see-through! You see, some dresses are crafted from lightweight pineapple cloth, made from pineapple leaf fibers. Those dresses usually have a partial lining and wide necklines.

The ladies help me wriggle into the two pieces. As is customary, Sally expertly hand stitches the bodice to the skirt. It must be done every time the dress is worn.

If I were a lady in the house, I would probably have worn a pair of bracelets with wire mesh bands and fancy sliders. Fashionable at the time, they were worn as matched sets, like earrings.

While I was dressing, Julie went over the game plan for our next move. Later, it may be a difference-maker that Sally overheard it all. She's a wild card, after all.

"I spoke to Virginie, told her you're a seamstress looking for room and board, and she's agreed to let you stay in the attic in exchange for sewing work," she says. "Virginie likes the fact that you'll be available anytime for, um, fashion emergencies. True, it's hot as hell up there, but it's better than nothing. We'll go up as soon as you return."

The decision had been made without me. I am grateful.

"I feel so much better that you have your bed back – and your privacy," I admit. "You've been so good to me. How can I ever repay you?"

"You'd do the same for me. I know it." She's right.

Julie studies me in my finished state of dress, and then rifles through her jewelry box until she finds a cameo made of carved shell. She leans over to place the pin at the neckline, saying cheerfully, "Now, that looks better!"

Sally pulls out a miser's purse with a slit in the middle and two slider rings to close off each end, so money won't fall out. She hangs the purse from my belt. Julie generously adds precious coins, enough to buy a pastry and coffee. Café du Monde won't open until 1862; no beignets for now.

Before leaving Julie's room, Sally hands me a bonnet. It's reminiscent of the white circular hat described in *The Handmaiden's Tale* to offset all the red garb. The bonnet she gives me is more practical than the more recently debuted "spoon bonnet," which is open and frames the face without offering much protection from the sun. Suntans, Julie reminds me, are not stylish.

Julie pushes toward me a pair of clunky black shoes to try on. Other than a slight pinch, which I know will irritate with every step, the shoes fit well enough.

So, the daily routine will go like this: breakfast with Julie, accompanying Sally to clients' homes, returning to my new "penthouse" apartment, and waiting for Julie to bring me a dinner plate, since I'm not allowed in the dining hall at night. If it's not too muggy, I may fall asleep for a few hours. At least until my predicament is over, I have a purpose.

That afternoon, Marie bypasses the staff and Madame's room and heads straight to the attic to wash my hair. How did she know where I was already?

"How are you feeling?" she asks. She makes polite chit-chat for a moment, then jumps directly to the point. "Let's get down to business, shall we? Tell me what you were doing before you got here."

"Well," I start lamely, careful to remember the outline. "My husband was working, and I took care of our home."

"Marie is unimpressed. I know she wants information on the power players."

"Who's mayor of New Orleans?"

"Tanya Cantrell."

"Is she white?"

"No, she's black."

"Well, I'll be!" she shrieks with laughter. "Do people like her?"

"They tolerate her. When a woman died during a Mardi Gras parade in 2019 by getting pulled under a float, Mayor Cantrell stopped the parade. For good. Krewes were mad about that. They'd invested a lot of money in "throws." She made all floats going forward have some special safety device that was in very short supply. Floats without them were out of luck. Mardi Gras was over."

"How is she about business?"

"Pretty shameless. She has her pet projects, the ones that benefit her. Like those Blue Bikes she's pushing. Independent bike dealers be damned. Parking lots were redone to make room for only her bikes. Truly, she's probably a fine person, but just like any other self-serving politician."

I see Marie's wheels spinning. She's not interested in minutia.

"Who's governor?"

"John Bel Edwards just won reelection."

"Was Huey Long ever elected governor?"

"Not Huey Long, Sr. But yes, Huey Long, Jr. was governor." I recall he ruled Louisiana from 1928 to 1932.

Nicknamed "The Kingfish," Junior was arguably the crookedest politician of his time. He drew on deep reservoirs of allies to take forceful action. After he served his term, he spent three years in the U.S. Senate before he was assassinated.

"He was killed? I knew his granddaddy," Marie mumbles. "He was a rascal. Didn't care who he screwed over. His arrogance was his downfall. Besides, he owed me a couple of favors that I didn't get a chance to cash in on. I see my curse on his family worked."

Is it true that her curse worked? Or did she just take credit?

Marie continues peppering me with questions.

"What about a World's Fair? Has New Orleans had one yet?"

I thought it was an odd question until I realized world's fairs had been going on since 1791. In 1861, the buzz was about four spread-out events – in Brisbane, Queensland; Melbourne, Victoria; Metz, France; and Amsterdam, Netherlands.

"Yes, in 1984." Should I mention the daily fireworks along the riverfront, 70,000 helium balloons released, politicians and doomsday preachers roaming the streets, kissing babies, and speaking from every street corner? Or that MGM swimming phenomenon Esther Williams made an appearance? She probably doesn't care about any of that. Minimal details, I remind myself.

Marie runs down her mental list to the next disconnected item.

"Who's running Brennan's?"

Brennan's? Another odd question.

"I'm not quite sure. I assume it's family."

In 1861, Owen Brennan operates the uber popular Old Absinthe House on Bourbon. He sells international foods, tobaccos of all sorts, and exotic wines. Marie frequents the place when she wants to hold court. But she had one bad experience she won't speak of.

"I put a curse on that Brennan family. Nothing ever went wrong?"

"It did."

Marie's ears perk up.

"The restaurant changed family hands quite a bit. Back in 1973, when Ted Brennan died, the family split. The widow and her children ran Brennan's on Royal. His siblings and their children owned Brennan's other restaurants in New Orleans, Houston, and Dallas."

"Houston? Dallas?" Marie seemed oblivious to those locations, even though Houston, Texas was founded in 1836; Dallas, Texas in 1841. Few New Orleanians were aware of goings-on outside the center of their world.

I ignore her and return to my story. "Then, a few things soured the restaurant. A monster storm, Hurricane Katrina, hit New Orleans in 2005. The contents of their second-story refrigerators melted onto lower floors and the wine cellar lost temperature control. Their entire wine collection was ruined."

Marie smirks.

"But there was never any financial trouble other than that?"

"Yes, around 2013, a cousin of the former owners bought Brennan's for a steal at auction. It took a year of extensive renovation before it reopened."

Marie snickers, satisfied.

It's time to turn the tables. I'm feeling bold. "Tell me, Marie, what does the Pool of Souls mean to you?"

Marie leans forward, eyes wide. "How do you know about that?"

"The Pool of Souls has some historical significance, but I'm not sure what," I elaborate. I don't tell her the Pool of Souls has become a clothing-optional community with a whip chamber, chains, and a nooky room. Late on weekend nights, the pool rocks with naked people in various forms of canoodling, music blasting to the dismay of residents at the adjoining Saint Pierre condominiums.

Marie hesitates, mulling whether to tell me the truth. "The Pool of Souls ... is a bridge between our worlds. It's a portal to different times."

"Will it help me get home to Parker?" I'd told her the sob story of missing my husband.

"It could. I'll show you where it is sometime soon," she said, patting her thighs in the rocking chair before standing up. "If you help me get what I want, I'll help you get home."

I could tell it was going to take a while before that happened. Unless I could steer the conversation elsewhere, she had me trapped, funneling information to her until it ran out. Then I would be useless. Would I ever get home?

"Parker has access to the Internet," I blurt out.

"The Internet?" Marie's brows furrow. "What's that?"

"It's a way to communicate with just about anybody and also have instant access to just about any information," I explain poorly.

Marie is intrigued.

"Yes, Parker can be quite useful, but I must get in touch with him."

After a beat, Marie surprises me by grabbing my arm and guiding me out of the room. I guess my nasty hair can wait.

"I'll take you to the Pool of Souls now, and you can talk to your man. I'll show you how to dream together. I have many questions for him."

Marie rushes down the stairs, dragging me by the hand, and pushes through the passageway and turns northwest toward Rampart Street. We pass by the carriage factory located next door, on the corner of Rues Toulouse and Burgundy, whose sad-looking industrial landscape is my view from the attic, and whose foul odors saturate the atmosphere. We pass by the nation's first cotton press, later a sheet metal company, that occupies the space where Maison Dupuy now stands. After turning northeast on Rampart, we pass by several homeless people until we stop at 628 in front of a solid black door with a heavy door knocker and no other form of identification. It looks as sketchy then as now.

Marie knocks on the door and is immediately ushered in. She has clout, that woman. The corridor winds around tropical plants and exotic birds to a dumpy-looking shanty. A red-bricked wall rises eight feet above the ground, sheltering a black-bottomed garden pool bordered by stacked stones and palm trees.

I know this much about the storied block: Beginning around 1743, the French Quarter dead were buried in the square encircled by Rampart Street and Rues Saint Peter, Toulouse, and Burgundy. It was a dumping ground; bodies had been piled on top of each other for decades. The legend goes that some of those souls looked for a way out. When this natural spring was discovered, it became a place for souls to pass through.

But I play dumb about that knowledge.

I follow her obediently to the pool and follow her instructions. I remove my shoes, step in, and let the coolness wash over me. I close my eyes to the sunlight and spread my arms wide.

"Keep your eyes closed," Marie warns, joining me in the pool and taking my hand. She begins chanting in a deeply guttural tone.

I keep my eyes tightly shut. She begins in a whisper and crescendos to a thunderous roar. The wind gusts, picking up speed as she raises her voice to what sounds like gibberish. Just when it starts to get scary, Marie dramatically drops her voice.

"Let Parker Bevilaqua's presence be known," Marie commands the sky.

With that statement, the air stills. Marie is quiet. All that can be heard is the sound of tinkling water. Even the birds are silent. At first, nothing. Then faintly, I hear a familiar voice. "Cici! Cici!"

Even though I promised not to, I open my eyes to an overwhelming, glaring brightness. I feel the warmth of Parker's arms around me, hugging me tightly.

"Oh, Cici! I was so worried about you! I love you! I've missed you! Thank God you're back!"

I can't see Parker. I hug back, savoring the moment.

Then suddenly, Parker disappears, the sky turns dark, and so does my world.

Chapter 19

Mardi Gras

March 4, 1862

SUNLIGHT CREEPS SLOWLY across the undressed attic windows until I saunter out of bed. I need energy for this busy day. I'm in a well-practiced routine. Time for releasing the early morning pee into the wild. Fortunately, not many people walk beneath these windows.

Next, it's time to "garb up," with all those loose layers of cotton voile and undergarments. With the flourished twist of a bow on my bonnet, I head downstairs for breakfast with Julie. I'm allowed in the dining hall only for the morning meal. Breakfast is a la carte, with people munching on pastries, nuts and fruits, and dried meats. Fresh eggs might be on the menu for us lesser folks if the backyard hens laid enough. Lunch at the mansion is somewhat informal if there are day guests. Dinnertime is sacredly formal for the family. That's ok. I'm appreciative of what I can get. Julie brings me platters of leftovers at night.

At the breakfast table, Julie is chattier than usual. The discussion is all Mardi Gras. Tomorrow will be Ash Wednesday. It'll be interesting to see how both days are celebrated during the antebellum war years.

Mimi is listening intently to Julie's tentative plans and speculation about how the growing prevalence of Union troops may hinder Mardi Gras festivities. An air of tentativeness permeats the French Quarter.

"I wanna go!" Mimi interjects, after hearing treats will be tossed to parade goers.

"No, Mimi, this isn't a day for children to be on the streets," Julie replies with a heavy sigh, as if she's too often repeated the same response.

I pick up a croissant roll, dab it with fruit butter, sprinkle a few pecans, and munch on bacon smoked over cherrywood. I pour a small glass of orange juice and settle in for conversation.

"Juls, what do you plan to do first today?" I ask.

"I'm not sure. The word is to wait until later in the day to decide, when the sun starts going down," she says. "What are your plans, Cici?"

"I have a fitting for Sally, over at the mayor's wife's home," I start.

"Oh, that's right. What has the mayor's wife been discussing lately?"

"I don't know. I haven't been there for several weeks. If I hear anything of importance, I'll let you know."

Julie brightens when sharing plans to paint palm trees in the courtyard until mid-afternoon. The weather is mild; the temperature should reach the mid-sixties. Then she'll reconsider the timing of getting dressed for whatever Mardi Gras merriment is to be had.

I gulp down the remaining orange juice, having pleased my belly with good food, and rise a little too quickly to depart the room. The back of my legs catches on a chair that refuses to budge over a loose floor plank and I stumble. I try to recover from that woozy blunder with some grace and dignity. Julie laughs.

"What a silly way to start the day," I joke, making a funny face to Mimi's delight. I say my goodbyes, gather my sewing supplies and an umbrella, and head downstairs.

The trek to Mayor Thomas Overton Moore's French Quarter residence involves traveling four blocks toward the Mississippi River and two blocks toward Canal Street. I keep my eyes alert, expertly dodging trails of sewage being dumped from windows above.

On Rue Toulouse, a parade of street criers hawks their late winter produce: a diverse assortment of asparagus, broccoli, cabbage, carrots, cauliflower, collards, garlic, lettuce, onions, spinach, strawberries, tangerines, and turnips.

Peddling crops is street theater, particularly during the fall harvest season of artichokes, bananas, cantaloupes, green peppers, snapbeans, oranges, and watermelons. Young blacks frequently work in pairs, each carrying baskets of produce and lyrically announcing their arrival in an early version of rap. One seller attracts my attention: an elderly French woman at the reins of a mule-pulled, decrepit, squeaky wagon brimming with fruits and vegetables. She stops at each house to announce her menu.

Another vendor gives me pause. Last summer, a smallish man with a balding head covered by a stiff cowboy hat cupped his hands around his mouth, bellowing "Watermelons! Watermelons! Red to the rind watermelons!" Behind him, he dragged a wagon chock full of green and white zebra-striped melons, with one halved to show the fruit was truly red to the rind. Today, he's back hawking collard greens, his blue eyes sparkling with excitement.

This vendor reminds me of my grandfather. I remember hearing tales about him growing watermelons on his south Mississippi farm and selling them in the French Quarter, and his dad and granddad before that. Could this man be related? No, that's not possible. Or is it?

Past the procession of carts, I see glimmerings of early partying. Celebrants, in various stages of inebriation, wear masks with the most colorful clothing they possess, no matter how tacky, and wave banners in the air with abandon. One of them hurls as I pass by, but fortunately, I anticipated it and skirted the fracas.

When I arrive at the mayor's residence, he's leaning back in a studded black leather chair in his study at the front of the residence, feet propped on the vast ornamental desk. His presence is imposing, with a high forehead, wide eyes, and half-pie eyebrows. His nose appears Greek; his lips are thin. But his hair! He keeps a sweeping thick mane of blondish tresses brushed away from his heart-shaped face, which offsets a full beard that starts at his chin and falls several inches beneath. Overall, his "lion face" is model-worthy.

Moore, a Presbyterian Democrat, was elected in 1860 and supplied 8,000 soldiers to the Confederate States of America – 5,000 more than Confederacy President Jefferson Davis requested. But none of that will matter when

Navy ships overtake Confederate boats in less than two months. Moore will see his plantation burn to the ground, escape to Mexico and then Cuba, and somehow receive a full pardon before his death in 1876.

But for today, we're pandering to Bethiah Leonard, the mayor's wife. She's rather large and unpleasant, with orange ringlets that morph into dreads, and a nasty case of rosacea. Tomorrow is hair washing day, or so I'm told. As usual for these fittings, she's holding finger foods in both hands. She speaks loudly and gravitates to bold colors that don't suit her. Sally warned me to go with what the mayor's wife wants, not what looks flattering.

"Well, hello there, Cecilia Bevilaqua!" Bethiah cries enthusiastically. Unfortunately, overpronouncing my name elicits a great deal of spit. As I approach her, I duck with a curtsy to avoid being showered. "What are we looking at today? New sketches, perhaps? Hmm?"

From a tattered notebook, I pull out three sketches for ball gowns for a charity event scheduled close to Easter. The ball will be held at the antebellum mansion of John Hampden

Randolph, a prestigious sugar cane farmer who built Nottoway, a luscious 31-acre plantation. Society favorites are eager to capture a glimpse of its tennis courts, fitness center, bowling alley, and two honeymoon suites – and to test its flushing toilets.

In the last six months, silhouettes of the crinoline have changed slightly. Instead of being dome-shaped, the skirt now flattens at the front and projects out the back, mimicking a big caboose. With Union soldiers arriving daily, there's debate on whether ball gowns should be black, as in mourning for the Confederacy.

Looking over the sketches with greasy fingers, Bethiah shrieks loudly with glee: "I like all three sketches!" From the front room, the mayor barks, "Choose one!"

Bethiah frowns, and then whispers. "Ok, maybe just two. Show me the fabric samples."

I gather black silk taffeta with matching glass beads and velvet ribbon. I explain the undersleeves will be made of cotton net, the bodice lined with polished cotton, and the skirt faced with black polished cotton.

"Oh, let me feel it!"

She grasps the taffeta, soiling it with grease. Her eyes glaze over when I mention details of the skirt: three rectangles of fabric, cartridge pleated to a waistband. It's all worn over a Victorian chemise, drawers, a red corset, cage crinoline, and a petticoat. But when I mention the necklace for this gown is a strand of graduated black glass beads and the hairpiece would consist of flowers twisted together with floral wire, she perks up.

"Let's definitely hold onto this one," she says, while licking her fingers.

Bethiah instantly dismisses a flattering fabric sample that mimics pinkish floral stripe wallpaper. It includes a bodice with hand sewn lace, a single box-pleated skirt, and an eyelet petticoat. It's trimmed with piping in most seams and bodice linings. On the back is a row of tidy buttons that takes two pairs of hands to manage. To be honest, it was a throwaway sketch.

Bethiah brightens at an illustration of a very military-influenced ballgown in a colorful silk taffeta with a wide notched collar and bell sleeves. It's offset by a white cameo-pinned ascot and bright white gloves. Three tiers of black lace encircle the skirt. It's a stand-out gown befitting her station but isn't pleasing to her voluptuous figure.

She settles on both gowns, reasoning she'll wear black if Union soldiers overtake New Orleans before Easter, and the boldly colored one if not. She would ask forgiveness from her husband later. In the meantime, I ask forgiveness of the Lord for the curse words that will undoubtedly spring to mind while I measure her.

Other than making a few, expected disparaging remarks about her rivals, and trying to find out what they'll wearing, Bethiah didn't share much gossip. She seems distracted, even when her unruly son darts in and out of the room, stopping briefly to hide under her skirts and messing up the marked measurements.

After departing the mayor's residence, I mull walking upriver to the French Market. Fred Koeniger plans to open the Original Café du Monde Coffee Stand this year, but I don't know when. The Morning Call will rival Café du Monde when it opens in 1870. Interestingly, Acadians from Nova Scotia brought the popular recipe for doughnuts without a center to New Orleans. I can hardly wait to sip dark-roasted, chicory coffee, and inhale lavishly sprinkled French doughnuts. I giggle, remembering Parker and I often asked for double confectioner's sugar on those tasty beignets.

After stopping by a local favorite deli and grabbing a sandwich and tea, I head instead to the north side of Canal Street to what's now home to Woldenberg Park. Boats are so jam-packed; one could skip deck to deck well past the Mississippi River bridge. It's a sight to see when wharf rats – the real kind and how the homeless people at the docks are described – scatter when a boat leaves its station.

I munch while listening to a lone Scottish bagpiper in the same place where the stunning Mother River statue will later stand. I recognize the music as "Loch Lomond," a Jacobite song. At first listen, it sounds romantic. Instead, the lyrics describe the unsuccessful Catholic

Jacobite Uprising of 1745 against the Protestant English. On Mardi Gras, merriment takes many forms.

While walking back, I fondly recall connecting with Parker at the Pool of Souls last August, with the help of Marie. I'd fallen into his strong, warm arms at our first, very quick meeting. The second meeting took place a few weeks later, this time in a dream. Marie had summoned powers from the nether regions to allow us to dream in sync.

"Are you ok?" was Parker's first question.

"Yes, as well as can be expected for now, but I miss home. I miss you," I reply. Then I flip the question.

"I'm ok. It's weird with your comatose body next to mine, but I'm so glad we connected," he says. "I didn't know what to think. How did you get there?"

"I don't know. I fell asleep and landed here, the same place just 157 years earlier."

"Did you take a bunch of pills?" He knew the answer.

"Yes. I'm very ashamed."

"Did you just want to get away from me?"

"No, I wanted a break from life. I wanted to join Izzy."

"Do you want to come back? Are you happier there?"

"I'm happy to be going in the direction of getting home to you, which is what Marie promises. That's my only goal. If you'll have me."

"Of course, I want you back! How will you get back home?"

"I don't know. We need to figure that out. Let's meet at the Pool of Souls at noon Saturday." That's the only day Sally lets me rest. And it's forbidden to go anywhere except church and to visit family on Sunday. Someone's always watching.

Thunder and lightning interrupt my dreams, and I couldn't reconnect that night with Parker. I also couldn't decide if our conversation was real or imagined, but regardless, I felt much better the next day.

Our Saturday plans went awry when Parker couldn't get into the facility. A raucous swingers' party had taken over the pool. He'd forgotten it was Naughty 'n' Nawlins weekend, an annual sexual lifestyle convention that attracts thousands of horny people from every edge of the world. Language barriers don't matter for this event. Convention goers parade down Bourbon in various forms of undress, carrying pineapples that signify an open lifestyle and wearing studded black leather, while holding signs ranging from "Monogamy isn't natural!" to "Hedonism is humanism: make love, not war!"

Unfortunately, Parker and I didn't make contingency plans for our date, and I didn't know when we'd meet again.

We met by chance in a dream a few weeks later, and at the Pool of Souls on a quieter Saturday. Only a couple of tatted people were milling around the water, and it didn't matter that Parker spoke to "me." They glanced at him sideways once and then ignored him. New Orleans is such a crazy place that behavior of his sort is somewhat normalized.

Months ago, I curried favor with Marie Laveau with the October 2 accurate prediction of the damning hurricane. As a result, she ramped up communications with Parker, but now wants more information in return. So far, she's allowed us to talk freely. Parker and I have discreetly decided how to best handle her questions in a way that keeps me safe and draws me closer to home.

Because I didn't have another household to call on, I headed to the Pool of Souls to visit Parker. We had agreed to Mardi Gras day at 3 o'clock in the afternoon, when the magnificent tier of clock bells at Saint Louis Cathedral would ring.

I arrive with little trouble; he did, too. The Pool of Souls was uncharacteristically quiet for such an important holiday. But storms are brewing. The way we "visit" involves looking deep inside the rings of the pool's reflection and finding not our own images but each other's. We waited for a light rain shower to pass. Then it was clear again. But what Parker had to say was deeply disturbing.

"Cici, there's a deadly airborne disease coming this way," he starts. "A strain called coronavirus allegedly started in a food market in Wuhan, China, and there's no cure."

Parker explains how this variety has an incubation period of 14 days. Mardi Gras in 2020 took place February 25. He had joined the ruckus on Canal Street, competing shoulder-to-shoulder among thousands of inebriated celebrants for Krewe-tossed loot from elaborate floats.

"There's no reported case in Louisiana ... yet," he says. "But it'll take until March 11 to make sure."

Goosebumps roll across my arms and legs. This cannot be true! For once, I hope Parker is being overly sensational about a much lesser problem.

"What does this mean?"

"You might not be able to come home."

Chapter 20

Panic

I'M NOT SURE WHAT HAPPENED on the night of Mardi Gras. I'd carefully made my way home unnoticed and climbed the 96 twisting steps to my little cubbyhole. I spent the rest of the evening to myself, except when Julie brought in dinner late.

"Juls, I have disturbing news," I say, before she can close the door. "This afternoon, Parker told me about a worldwide pandemic making its way to New Orleans, a plague that could wipe out everyone. It's a highly contagious virus, like yellow fever, except it doesn't come in waves. It comes at once and seemingly swallows the earth."

For Julie, who had been dancing in the streets, the information was sobering.

"What does that mean?" she asks, settling into a rocking chair by a window. From there, she can see fireworks brightening the sky.

"It means there may not be a home to go back to." When I say it out loud, I'm frightened. It's real. There's no ignoring my plight.

"How will you know? When?"

I explain to Julie what Parker told me.

"Keep in mind that Parker tends to exaggerate. Our family always jokes to take what he says and divide it by four. I'm hopeful he's overreacting."

Julie shakes her head. "What would you do?"

Good question. I'd been planning to return to Parker's arms since I fell down the rabbit hole. I hadn't thought of another possibility.

"Could I stay here? Or is this hospitality a short-term basis?"

"I don't know. Virginie seems to like you and appreciates your work. She likes having someone at her beck and call. How long could it last? I don't know."

"What are my other options? I'm too old to marry. I'm past the age of bearing children. I'm even too old to be a prostitute!" I joke, but the subject isn't funny. "Where do people like me typically go?" Heck, I'm past the average life span of 46 years in the mid-1800s.

"Usually, their family cares for them, but you're neither family – nor Creole." Julie lowers her head.

"And what happens to those without families?"

"Um, I don't know. I haven't paid enough attention. Let's think about it for a minute." I have a feeling that Julie knows exactly what happens but doesn't want to worry me needlessly.

I plop in an adjacent rocking chair, admiring the glimmering light show, and we brainstorm.

"You must tell Marie," Julie decides. "She can help if you continue to help her. What kinds of questions is she asking Parker?"

"A lot of it is catch-up history. She wants to know what happened in the world wars and who's in charge. She's amazed that Queen Elizabeth is still on the throne, after 74 years. Queen Victoria didn't last that long, and it seemed forever at the time of her reign."

"Marie must have something in mind but doesn't want to tip her hand. Marie is a big thinker. Quite ambitious. Perhaps she simply wants to strengthen her powers."

We rock several minutes in silence until Julie has an idea.

"Sally may know of something. Do we know where she lives? Have you been to her place?"

"No."

"We should see her soon. If you make enough money, you can afford rent and groceries somewhere fairly safe."

"True, but how long can I sustain it? My hands are already arthritic. Is there a good possibility I'll be homeless?" I could feel my throat clamp down and a red flush cross my chest.

"I hope not! Let me mull this over tonight and we'll talk in the morning."

"Are you going back out to celebrate?"

"No, I'm done for the evening. I had my fun."

"I'm sorry to have interrupted it."

"It's fine. Ash Wednesday will do that soon enough."

Chapter 21

Dumbfounded

"MARIE, PARKER HAS TERRIBLE NEWS, and I don't know what to do," I start, hoping she'll have ideas to save me.

I know, I know. Needing Marie Laveau's help puts me at a distinct disadvantage.

"What on earth can it be, child?"

"Parker told me a terrible infection is spreading over the world and that I might not have a home to go back to."

"What is it?"

"A pandemic, he says. It's a highly contagious disease that started in Asia and is spreading rapidly. He says it has a 14-day window of incubation, which makes it extremely dangerous. It's almost undetectable."

Marie, who'd seen many bouts of yellow fever breakouts, was oddly unmoved. She'd witnessed many public health crises, including cholera, dysentery, smallpox, and tuberculosis. Through it all, she was in the trenches, aiding the sick and comforting the dying.

"I've seen bad things before and I can tell you that it'll pass," she reasons. "The good Lord doesn't want to start all over."

"If I can't go home, what will I do?"

"You'll continue preparing to go home. An opportunity will open up. I'm sure of it."

"But in the meantime ..."

"Stop panicking. That'll serve no one. I'm sure this is devastating to you, but we'll get through it."

I study Marie's face for sincerity. I want to believe everything she says to be true, but there's a pit in the bottom of my stomach that gives me pause.

"Make sure you connect with Parker often, and find out everything you can about this ... what is it?"

"Coronavirus," I say, trying hard not to chuckle. It sounds like a beer disease. But it's serious business. I admonish myself for poking fun at a fatal infection.

Marie begins rattling off instructions. "Cici, find out about stock market trends. What's hot? What's not? Especially now."

I'm shocked. How does an uneducated woman who can barely read and write know about the stock market? Then I remember the first stock market began in Amsterdam in 1611. The London Stock Exchange, the world's first major stock market, was established in 1698. America joined the fray in the late 1700s to invest money in company stock or government bonds. It's an old, well-oiled machine.

"I'll let you know," I promise.

When I see Sally later in the day, she also has input.

"I can keep you busy as long as business is good. But with Union soldiers bearing down, I don't know what that will mean for my Confederate clients. If Union soldiers burn down houses and run people out of town, we'll lose all our business. They'll go after the social elite, for sure."

"What will you do if that happens?"

"I'll probably move back to Philadelphia. I left business there, and Union women need to be dressed."

"Maybe I could go with you?"

"I don't think so. I have helpers. In fact, they're minding the business while I'm in New Orleans."

My outlook is growing dimmer. Then an idea occurs to me. I'm eager to get Julie's opinion. Mimi may need a tutor, or at least piano lessons. The piano teacher who comes by the house once a week is a lecherous, predatory chap who sidles too closely on the piano bench with such a young child. I also make a pretty good babysitter.

"We've discussed going to Paris until the war is over," Julie confides. "Virginie, our mother, Mimi and me. If that happens, I think you could come with us. Mimi will not need to neglect her studies. And she's too natural a piano player to stop taking lessons."

It bodes well for me that I played the piano and studied French. But if I tag along to Paris, I'll be running away from home for good. Once, I was willing to leave behind my family and friends in favor of darkness. Now, I don't want to go.

Chapter 22

The Day the Earth Stood Still

March 19, 2020

ON MARCH 19, 2020, the U.S. State Department raised its global travel advisory to level 4, effectively banning all international travel. Americans are, for the most part, sequestered in their homes. Roadways are eerily empty. Even the uber-busy Atlanta roadways appear ghostly.

By April 6, New Orleans was the epicenter of the deadly virus in the United States. So far, Parker hasn't been infected.

"Do you remember Gayfock?" Parker asks during a Pool of Souls meeting. We'd come up with a nickname for the despicable character who set up camp two doors down from our apartment.

"You mean that nasty, older neighbor who's hard of hearing and has boys traipsing through day and night?"

"Yeah, that guy. He's almost deaf. He's dragged his TV into the courtyard and talks on the phone all day long. It's so loud; I can hardly hear myself think. He's constantly throwing coronavirus parties. No masks."

I roll my eyes.

The problem is, Parker cannot access our apartment without passing Gayfock's. Parker's polite reminders to remain indoors and greatly limit guests have been ignored. Instead, the asking seems to have spurred him on. Now, he's dragged outside his stereo system. Plus, he's having his condo extensively remodeled to new ceiling heights, with all the bells and whistles. Workers parade in and out of his residence at all hours of the day. Boy toys come at night, bearing friends. Parker is an avid mask wearer; Gayfock's entourage repels them.

"Have you talked to Lisa?"

Lisa Garvey is the unreachable, absentee POA president. Even though she lives next door, she's a slippery soul. Some say she's in Europe; others say she's taken a place in California. Either way, her lack of interest leaves us in an unenviable position. How can we protect ourselves? The property management company, the lamest I've ever seen run a condominium complex, won't even take calls. It sounds preposterous – totally unacceptable – to shirk basic duties but the truth is, the situation is being repeated throughout the French Quarter. Locals know that calls to the NOPD or the health department are fruitless, no matter what the public service announcements say.

Parker is considering moving my comatose body to a safer place, but where is the prickly question. With the rising number of infections, hospitals are not safe. And if he moves me, how will I ever find him? What if the feeding tubes get tangled? Dr. Barkley is becoming more and more unavailable, for good reason.

When I give her an update, Marie Laveau remains unfazed.

"Surely, herbal medicine could cure this pandemic," she claims. But here's a worry about her theory: For all the lives Marie has saved, nothing can undo the seeming curse that envelopes her ovaries. According to different accounts, only two of her children reached adulthood. Was it by sickness or choice?

Her optimism seems out of place.

Sally interrupts our conversation with an urgent message to return to Bethiah Leonard's home. Apparently, she wants to discuss accessories for the second gown she contracted. But when I arrive, I'm asked to wait in a chair outside the mayor's office. As I sit down, I notice several agitated men standing over a desk with a map. It's April 18, and military strategy rumors are running amok.

"Captain Farragut's a gambler," a military man tells the mayor. "His plan won't work."

Captain David Dixon Farragut, a 60-year-old commander of the navy fleet, was a veteran of the War of 1812 and the Mexican War, and the naval counterpart of the army's Robert E. Lee. Farragut concocted a plan to level Fort Jackson and Fort Saint Phillip downriver from

New Orleans. He would then move upriver and turn his fleet of 17 war ships on the city. The forts are on opposite sides of the river, and more substantial than Union troops realize, a mayoral aide points out. To slow down the ships and make them vulnerable to attack, Confederate soldiers plan to place a chain across the river with sections between floating hulks.

"General (Mansfield) Lovell only has 3,000 troops," another military type emphasizes. Lovell is a major general in the Confederate States Army. "The forts are manned by only 1,100 men. There's upwards of 18,000 unprotected men under Butler at Ship Island." Butler is a major general in the Union Army.

Already, annual import trade on the Mississippi River has shrunk from nearly $156 million pre-war to barely $30 million by 1862.

"We're doomed," says another, covering his eyes. At that point, one of the elders notices me and unceremoniously slams the double doors shut.

I never saw the mayor's wife. That day, Farragut began 96 hours of firing 13,000 shells that left the forts intact. On the morning of April 24, Farragut gave orders to advance until New Orleans was left undefended.

When New Orleans was taken by land several days later, Butler, a Massachusetts man, was placed in charge of Louisiana. His reputation as a tyrant is legendary. Some called him "The Beast" for his extreme directives. He earned another nickname, "Spoons Butler," because of his fetish for stealing silverware.

In one of his first acts, Butler made an example of Confederate gambler William Mumford, who publicly tore up the newly planted U.S. flag and distributed bits and pieces of fabric to a crowd that egged him on. Butler had Mumford tried and publicly hanged. He also issued Order 28, in which he declared that women insulting federal troops would be treated and punished as prostitutes. His actions spurred British Prime Minister Viscount Palmerston to lament, "an Englishman must blush to think that such an act has been committed by one belonging to the Anglo-Saxon race."

In the eight months he served as Commander of the Department of the Gulf, Butler maintained order by imposing censorship and closing down churches and Confederate-sympathizer newspapers. He imprisoned citizens suspected of sedition. Propaganda showed Butler had a benevolent side, providing relief for the destitute by feeding the hungry, hiring the unemployed, and ridding the city of yet another yellow fever epidemic by scrubbing filthy streets and quarantining where necessary. In reality, he was mean spirited. For example, he fed the poor beef that had been condemned unfit for human consumption.

Regardless, Butler became a political liability for the Lincoln administration, which had gone to great lengths not to alienate European powers. Nathaniel P. Banks took his place in December 1862, immediately reopening churches, freeing political prisoners, and returning property taken by the Union army. Camaraderie between Union soldiers and New Orleanians was encouraged, and after the fall of

Vicksburg in 1863, New Orleans' economy bounced back.

Of course, fear was rampant. Nobody knew the outcome. I quietly celebrated my fiftieth birthday on March 28.

For now, Julie and I compare notes. She reminds me about Saint John's Eve coming up June 23, and how that's a time to ask for favors from ancestors past.

"We need divine intervention," she says. "This may be it."

Chapter 23

Summoning Damballa

June 23, 1862

THE ANNUAL SAINT JOHN'S EVE celebration is all about summoning the Great Damballa. Marie Laveau will hold court during the celebration, and we want to see what happens. How is the question. Julie and I are giddy with anticipation.

"Marie starts making preparations immediately after Easter," Julie explains. "Details take careful planning; they must be exact."

The festival is in honor of John the Baptist, who was born six months earlier than Jesus Christ.

"At that time, Marie makes the rounds of those she wishes to invite and collects donations to cover expenses of the ceremony," says Julie. "Then, she retreats to her shack on the bayou, and barters for almost everything – food, live animals for sacrifice, drummers for the drum circle."

"So, it's a money-maker for Marie," I surmise.

"Uh-huh," Julie nods.

The day before Saint John's Eve, Marie, the only one permitted to do so, prepares ritual offerings: shrimp Creole, pulled pork, hopping john, dirty rice, and spoon bread, collard greens and fatback. Not a single grain of salt may come in contact with the food. Therefore, white rice and roasted pork are spiced with cayenne pepper, grits, and a dish called "amala," a brew of chopped okra stewed with corn meal.

"Amala's a greasy mess unappealing to the crowd as a whole, but supposedly decadent in the spiritual world," Julie notes.

White rum. There must be plenty for followers and spirits. Damballa guzzles white rum, Julie stresses.

The night before, to wholly receive the blessings of saints and spirits, devout followers take special herbal baths to rid themselves of negative energy and compromised spiritual vibrations. Modern-day, devotees attend a ceremony at the International House Hotel at 221 Camp Street, led by revered leader Sallie Ann Glassman.

The day of the celebration, Marie has her disciples set up a wood pile that will burn into a colossal bonfire. Tables are arranged with foods; chickens to be sacrificed are stowed in nearby cages. Drummers set up their circle, and guests start to arrive with gifts for Marie – flowers, candles, hair ribbons and hair dressing supplies, perhaps Voodoo dolls, potions, and gris gris bags. Followers know blue is her favorite color.

Julie had never attended a Saint John's Eve fete yet agreed to show me the way. Modern day, we would start on the Magnolia footbridge over Bayou Saint John, near Cabrini High School.

Not having landmarks to follow made the trek more difficult, but we trudged through swampland guided by torchlights, ever mindful of snakes and alligators and Union soldiers. As we grow closer to the commotion, we hide in a bamboo grove.

We arrive just as the celebration starts at 7 o'clock sharp. Marie, dressed in white from head to toe, takes her rightful place in the center of a semi-circle of the chosen few.

"In the name of the Father, and of the Son, and of the Holy Spirit," Marie says, while banging a stick on the ground three times.

"Amen!" the crowd roars.

"Faith, hope and charity," Marie says, hands outstretched to the heavens.

"Amen!"

With that, the ceremony truly begins.

Marie's lieutenants hand her supplies she'll need throughout the evening, such as a vial of holy water taken from the baptismal fount at her parish church earlier in the day.

The crowd softly recites anthems – Our Father, Hail Mary, and the Apostles' Creed – as Marie sprinkles the ground surrounding the ceremonial pyre with dried herbs, graveyard dirt, and a few drops of holy water. Then she douses it with kerosene.

Marie's underlings touch the ground three times and trace a cross in the ground with cornmeal, ground white eggshells, dust from a church, and more dirt from a graveyard.

Next, they spill water from a pitcher three times on the ground, saying "pou mo-ye" for the dead. Food is then placed at four points of the cross.

The cry "mange sec pou mo-ye!" signals dry eating for the dead.

"In this part of the ceremony," Julie recalls from hearsay, "saints and spirits convert food offerings and spilt blood into pure energy that's then used to grant requests and to bring wealth and success."

With offerings laid out, Marie sips rum, spitting it onto the wood pile.

"What's happening now?" I ask, unable to see clearly.

"Marie is lighting small white tapers and putting them in the center of food dishes," Julie whispers.

With a curtsy, Marie leans over the pyre and lights the fire, tossing yarrow into the fray to ward against evil. The crowd roars its approval, and the atmosphere turns to party mode. The drum circle takes center stage, rhythmically playing softly and slowly.

I've never heard layers of singing like I did that night. Julie explains the songs are sung in Creole, French, and English to call down saints and ancestors. Meanwhile, women are gathering specific varieties of plants, such as elder flowers, fennel, foxgloves, lemon verbena, mallows, laburnum, rue, rosemary, and the prized species of all: Saint John's wart. Drumbeats crescendo to a fever pitch and then abruptly stop.

"Oh, this is it!" Julie whispers, excitedly, as a hush falls over the crowd. "A spirit has overtaken a body. Everyone's waiting for this person to speak."

In a tone of voice that doesn't match the body, a spirit espouses instructions.

"I can't understand what's being said," I speak softly.

"It's spoken in a language I don't get," Julie mutters. "But the spirit is giving instructions to be carried out. Also, the spirits spot hexes placed on its inhabitants."

To cleanse the unclean spirits, a live chicken is passed overhead and touched to the palms and back of the spirit body's hands until it reaches Marie, who snaps the chicken's neck and slits its throat with a sharp knife. The chicken is discarded.

"The chicken cannot be eaten because negative energy has passed on to the chicken," Julie whispers.

As more spirits inhabit them, people ask favors and lay flowers and dollar bills at their feet to thank them for favors granted the preceding year.

"It's considered an honor to be touched by a spirit," Julie notes.

Summoning Damballa comes next. The fire climbs and expands as the drumming once again intensifies in rhythm and beat. White rum flows freely. The bonfire must be white-hot for Damballa to appear.

Marie grinds around the fire erotically, frightfully close to the flames, shirking one piece of clothing after another. The drums reach a fever pitch. Suddenly, a spark emerges from the bowels of the bonfire and a shape slowly morphs into an ominous white snake, tongue flickering wildly.

Damballa has arrived.

Marie, now completely naked, lowers her soul's armor and blends her essence with his until she disappears into an orgasmic singularity and becomes filled with the spirit. The crowd responds by caressing and undressing those closest to them. An all-out orgy.

I did a double take when Marie reappeared a few minutes later on her throne, caressing a white snake.

"How did she get there? I was watching the entire time!"

Julie ignores my comment and taps my arm. "Look over there!"

As Marie is fondling Damballa, an unexpected ally comes into sight. Sally is partially hidden by vegetation on the opposite side of the fire from Marie. The crowd parts enough for us to watch several people around her, one with hands up her left leg, another massaging her tatas, and yet another rubbing her shoulders. In one hand is a peace pipe. As the wind lifts her already scrunched-up skirt, the sight we see rattles us to the core. Suddenly, Marie's rituals take a back seat. Sally, as is obvious to both of us, is a hermaphrodite. A slightly built man rubs her exposed cock.

"So that's the big secret!" Julie whispers, a little too loudly.

"Shhh," I admonish her. We don't need unwanted attention.

It took a few minutes for us to make sense of it all. But one thing we didn't anticipate, other than the obvious, was Sally's kinship with

Marie, who has kept her secret safe. We never thought Sally and Marie traveled in the same social circles, much less the greatest celebration of the year for Voodooists.

"Have we said anything to Sally that she could've passed on to Marie?"

Of all things, words are our primary concern? I felt certain I'd complained to Sally about Marie here and there, thinking Sally and I were on the same page. Plus, she heard everything we discussed that first day I was being dressed. Now, this new truth puts the charade to the test. How far off-base have I been? Julie is as unnerved as me.

"Let's go," Julie says, grabbing my hand. "I want to get out of here. Now!"

We rush so quickly along the path home, jumping over tall weeds, sidestepping drunk partyers, and skirting piles of rugged rocks, that our dresses are tattered and our skirts muddied. That might take some explaining unless we can sneak into the mansion undetected.

As we make our way back home, we pass doorsteps piled high with ingredients combined to keep witches and evil spirits at bay. Green birch, long fennel, Saint John's wort, white lilies, and garlands of beautiful flowers are wrapped around oil-burning lamps.

When we arrive at the mansion, short of breath, Ollie lunges from the shadows.

"What have you ladies been up to?" he asks, incredulously.

"We've been on quite the adventure," Julie responds. "Please don't tell anyone."

"Miz Julie, your secrets are always safe with me." It was then I realized Ollie has a schoolboy crush on Julie the equivalent of Mimi's affections for Ollie.

Ollie pours water over the briar cuts on our legs and arms, followed by rubbing them with yarrow for its anti-inflammatory properties.

"I want to hear about it," Ollie says, "but not tonight."

Little did we know that someone was watching from above.

Chapter 24

Lacerated Wounds

JULIE AND I HAD attended the Saint John's Eve celebration with the sole intent of finding solutions to our problems. Instead, we found more trouble. Paranoia is paramount, though one concern was put to rest. Our voyeur was Mimi, who had slipped out of her bedroom to see what all the fuss was about. She was none too pleased to notice Ollie's likings toward Julie.

We need answers. Does Marie Laveau know we were there? Does Sally know we saw her and what we saw? In our ignorance of the process, did we garner negative spirits? What will become of us? What will become of me?

Two mornings later, Sally shows up unannounced. She knocks on my door as she enters.

"I have another client for you," Sally says, appearing unconcerned. I breathe a sigh of relief. "This one you'll like. It's Baroness de Pontalba, who built Pontalba Apartments next to the Saint Louis Cathedral and Saint Anthony Garden. She's a shrewd businesswoman and a highly regarded designer. And a Creole. She already has the material and the patterns ready for the gowns we need to sew."

"When is she expecting me?"

"This morning. She stays quite busy and has some business to tend to later today with her sons, she told me."

The Pontalba Apartment building replaced dilapidated row houses in the 1850s, becoming America's first official apartments. I've always wondered how they look on the inside, and now I have my chance. And I've been long fascinated by the baroness. I could hardly believe my luck. Even better, it's located across Rue Decatur from the French Market.

With a practiced eye, I walk down Rue Toulouse toward the river until turning left on Rue Royal. I pass the Saint Louis Cathedral before arriving at the revered building, which looks glorious in its newly built state.

I knock on No. 5, Rue Saint Peter, as instructed. Instead of a servant answering the door, it was the baroness, with voluminous almost-black, shoulder-length hair shaped around a pretty head, and bluish-gray eyes. She greets me warmly with a quick smile. She doesn't look like the "fiery redhead" as I'd heard described. Spanish by birth, French by marriage, and American upon Louisiana's admission to the Union, the baroness had defied all odds to even be alive.

When she was a toddler, Micaela Leonarda Antonia de Almonester Rouas y de la Ronde inherited a fortune – rumored to be half a million dollars at that time–from her Spanish father, Don Andres Almonaster y Rojas. After being raised by the Ursuline Sisters at the convent on Rue Chartres, her mother arranged a marriage in 1811, when she was 15, to a 20-year-old French cousin. It was obvious from the onset the marriage didn't take. Tired of being a virtual prisoner at the moated, medieval de Pontalba chateau in France, she moved to New Orleans and sought a divorce.

As divorce proceedings dragged on, and in an effort to steal her inheritance, her father-in-law, Baron de Pontalba, shot Micaela four times at point-blank range with a pair of dueling pistols and dragged her down the stairs. When she survived the attack, the baron turned a gun on himself and didn't miss. Though never divorced, she won the round of legal separation and two sons, Alfred and Gaston.

I knew the bullets had damaged her left breast and hand, and mutilated two fingers. I was apprehensive about measuring her, but she had already measured herself and thrust illustrations in my hands.

"This one is to wear to a social event here ... the other is to be worn in Paris, where I'm moving to," she points to each sketch. "The others, you can keep. Sally's always been good to me. Maybe they'll be useful."

In the sketch for the New Orleans gown, Micaela drew a bateau neckline with off-the-shoulder poufy short sleeves in a light lavender silk fabric. A broad lavender ribbon will accentuate her tiny waist. The easy style of the dress belies its discomfort.

On the baroness, fabric moves easily. For this event, her hair will be stacked on top, somewhat askew. Marie doesn't run in Baroness de Pontalba's circle, but her servants do. Perhaps that's why she answers her own door.

The baroness, a fashion icon, carries clout. Around the same time she built the fabulous four-story red brick building with lacy ironwork balconies for 50 residences, 10 retail stores, two restaurants and a coffee shop, she led a civic group to pressure municipal government to rename Place d'Armes "Jackson Square," in memory of Major General and President Andrew Jackson. City hall also granted her wish to convert Place d'Armes into a formal garden, giving Pontalba Apartment residents an impressive view that also spans the Mississippi River and Saint Louis Cathedral.

"I need it in two weeks," insists the baroness. "Will that give you enough time?"

"Yes, of course," I reply, knowing it's the only acceptable answer.

The next day, Sally sends me to Exchange Place, to a residence near the city's notorious fencing school. Julie was with me when Sally dropped by, and neither of us thought she knew that we know about her sexual imbalance.

Famous instructors Don Jose "Pepe" Llulla, Armant Robert Severin, and Basile Croquere were outside Exchange Place, teaching young, wealthy Creole men how to fence. They often dueled several times a day on the street outside the second-floor studio, which retains countless fence marks on its white-washed brick walls. "Quel lieu your se batter!" translates to "what a place for a fight!"

"Pepe" is known as the "greatest duelist who has a cemetery of his own," and credits his fencing success to lifelong abstinence from alcohol. Croquere is recognized as "the most remarkable colored fencing master of Louisiana," according to author Stuart Landry.

Croquere, educated in Paris, is known for his handsome looks, exquisite manners and charming personality, and skill as a dance master. When he isn't teaching as the finest fencing master in New Orleans, he is a stellar mathematician, teacher and carpenter who taught the sport to the cream of Creole society. Yet because of his race, he never fought a duel.

It is an honor to be in their presence, of course, at a distance.

Exchange Place, namely the Merchant's Exchange Building, had been established in 1835 by Anglo-Americans wanting to funnel more business to their comrades instead of Creoles. At the time, Canal Street was the dividing line between French Quarter Creoles and Central Business District Anglo-Americans. It strategically intersects with Canal Street and Rues Iberville and Bienville. Interestingly, it's also the home of the Sazerac. And sadly, it's also the alley where slaves have been moved like cattle from ships to the auction block at Saint Louis Hotel.

The lady of the house, who I was summoned to measure, was not at home. It took me a while to realize there was no client. I was being toyed with because Sally needed me out of the house. Paranoia burrows deep.

# # #

On Rue Toulouse in 2020, Parker awakes from a nightmare to hear helicopter rotors swirling above his head. Instead, it's a ceiling fan whirring at top speed. Tending to me has taken its toll. He's intent on keeping me safe from the pandemic and Gayfock types. Since I've been comatose, damage has been done to my body, despite Parker's efforts to turn me constantly to prevent bed sores.

"Parker, I don't know how long you can keep it up," Barkley told him last week. "It's getting more dangerous every day until someone comes up with a cure, or at least a vaccine. Who knows how long this will drag on, or if it'll take us all down? It's the darndest thing I've ever witnessed."

"I'm determined to do the best I can for Cici until the very last breath," Parker said. "Whether hers or mine. I can't live without knowing I've done everything possible to help her."

Parker didn't mention my double life, or the entrapment on both sides.

"Thanks, Dr. Barkley, for continuing to check in with me, knowing it's a difficult time for you, too." Parker genuinely means it.

"Something needs to happen soon, or we'll lose her," he warns.

Chapter 25

Tipping Point

ON THE WALK BACK from Exchange Place, my imagination runs wild. Why was I sent on a wild goose chase? What did Sally tell Julie? Where was Marie Laveau? I haven't seen her since Saint John's Eve.

I decide to take my chances at the Pool of Souls, to see if somehow, I can connect with Parker. Maybe he has good news. Just maybe.

I slip through the black door unnoticed, and meander to the back, happy to find no one there. I lean over the clear water in search of his face. After several minutes, a very tired, almost haggard-looking Parker is reflected to me.

"Parker, are you ok? You look wretched!"

"Um, thanks, Cici. I'm worn out and don't feel well."

My heart lurches. "Don't feel well? You don't have the virus, do you? Please say you don't."

"I don't have the virus. I just haven't been able to sleep because I'm watching over you," he admits. "I don't want anything to happen to you."

His statement gives me pause. Before I can comment, I hear a sharp crackle in the background. "What's that?"

"Yet another thunderstorm," he sighs. "They're calling for more flash flooding."

"Oh, Parker! Will it ever end?"

"I don't know, but last time it rained so hard, water came up to the threshold and almost flooded the apartment. NOLA Ready is warning this storm could get worse. They're asking everyone to park on the highest ground possible."

"What will you do if it floods the apartment?" I don't want to invite trouble, but we need to be prepared.

"People will be coming in and out, and I'll have a hard time keeping you hidden and safe."

"Everything sounds like doom and gloom," I lament, shaking my head.

"It hasn't happened yet," Parker reminds me. "Let me go, so I can take precautions. When it starts pouring, things get out of hand quickly. Just remember I love you."

"Take precautions, but please get some rest. You're no good to anybody if you're in bad shape, too. Sorry, but I get dibs on that."

Parker chuckles at my attempt at humor. And in a flash, he's gone, before I can respond, "I love you, too."

It's such a hot, balmy afternoon that I hike up my skirts, take off my Dutch shoes, and step lightly into the pool to cool off. But it feels there's no limit to the depth of the black-bottomedness and I quickly regain my footing on the edge. Hmm. What's this? Is there a secret portal I've stumbled onto? Is going home as easy as basically baptizing myself? I would have some explaining to do if I showed up at the mansion soaking wet. Steadying myself, I dip a toe into the pool, going as far down as my body will allow while continuing to keep my balance. I don't feel the bottom! I try to will Parker back into the picture, but he's gone.

I've seen people in the pool now and modern-day, and I've never seen a phenomenon like a bottomless pool. I study my surroundings. The part of the pool I've been "meeting" Parker in is almost a pool by itself. Could it be a coincidence? Or must certain elements be in place for the bottom to disappear? I cannot put my theory to the test right now. I'll have to think it through. Should I mention it to Marie? Or does Marie already know?

When I hear movement among the tropical plants, it's time to go. Maybe it's just a bird, but I cannot take the chance of seeing anyone right now. As I leave, I notice the noise is coming from a black crow. How odd.

I make my way back to the mansion, pondering the possibilities of a way to return home. Parker needs a break. This must end.

Chapter 26

Bargaining

I DROP BY THE HORSE STABLE long enough to pet Zelda and to say hello to Ollie, thanking him once again for saving me months ago.

"No trouble," he says, with an aw-shucks attitude.

I pass Fanny on the second floor, dangling her sweaty fat sausage arms. It's amazing how she always looks the same – haggard – whether at the beginning or end of a shift.

As I start to climb the second set of stairs to my bedroom, Julie grabs me and pulls me into her room. Marie Laveau is waiting in the rocking chair, arms crossed. This isn't good.

"Cici, Marie knows."

Puzzled, I look from one to the other for more information.

"Marie knows we were there on Saint John's Eve. She knows what we saw."

Marie remains frustratingly quiet.

"When Marie meets Damballa, she becomes the center of a spiritual field, and she sensed our presence."

"Oh, I see," I say, unconvincingly. "Does Sally know?"

"No," Marie heaves a deep sigh, "she does not know that you know her secret. She doesn't have the same powers. But she has pretty good intuition. How has she seemed to you?"

"The same. She sent me to Pontalba Apartments to pick up sketches and measurements from Baroness de Pontalba. But then ..."

"Then what?"

"But then she sent me to Exchange Place for a fitting, but no one was home," I say, looking at Julie, who shrugs her shoulders. I can tell Julie knows something she doesn't want to share. Something is amiss. Suddenly, I feel very uncomfortable.

"Don't worry," Marie says, soothingly, while uncrossing her arms. "It's not all that bad. So, you know how I summon my powers, and you saw me seduce Damballa. It's not a secret."

"Where does that leave us?"

"With more truth," Marie emphasizes. "Now you know how things work."

"Where does that leave us with Sally?"

Julie shifts awkwardly.

"Juls, sit down," Marie instructs. Julie obliges.

"Sally and I pretend to not get along, but we obviously do. She doesn't know that you were there unless she stumbled upon you herself. And for that one night, I don't think it matters what she was doing. Saint John's Eve is a sacred time, you see. Secrets are revealed and forgotten. Do you understand what I mean?"

I nod feebly.

"So that's that. We'll discuss it no more. Now on to more important matters. What's the latest with Parker?"

"He's fatigued. My comatose body isn't doing well. Time is running out."

"Then here's what we're going to do. Contact him again as quickly as you can and gather some information for me. I need more tools for …" Her voice trails off.

"He's having difficulty with a storm coming in and flooding and keeping up with me," I remark. "This might not be the best time to reach him."

"First, now is the only time to reach him," Marie says, as if there's no choice. "Second, it rarely floods in the French Quarter. It may seem that water's going to pour in, but it always skirts the edges. I'll make a way for you two to reach each other in your dreams tonight. We'll meet again tomorrow."

Marie stands up slowly, stretches her arms, curls her long fingers around her cane and heads out. Zombi stayed home again, thank goodness.

After hushed goodbyes, Julie returns to Marie's chair and plops down.

"We have a problem, Cici. It's Sally."

Chapter 27

Playbook

"SALLY WANTS TO MEET US," Julie whispers, as if speaking softly makes it less scary.

"Where? When? Why?"

"She wants to meet here tomorrow morning. I don't know why."

"What's going on?"

"I don't know. I really don't. It do know it's not about sewing. At least I don't think it is. But something about it seems, well, rather bizarre."

"When she sent me to Exchange Place, the lady I was supposed to see wasn't home. That's a first. I noticed she hung around here with you and assumed you two had talked."

"We talked a little about Virginie's newest day gown, but she seemed distracted. And she left quite abruptly."

Something smells funny. I remember seeing Julie and Sally huddled in deep, quiet conversation. What am I not being told? I decide to be bold.

"Juls, you and Sally were talking intimately when I left. I cannot believe it was about a dress. And she's never sent me to a place that didn't welcome me. What gives?"

"I thought she was going to tell me something of significance. She started to but didn't. I was playing along."

I'm unconvinced, but cannot exactly accuse her of lying, or at least omitting a crucial part of the truth. I guess I'll find out when Sally arrives.

It should be a societal rule not to give a paranoid person another reason to be paranoid. And definitely not to make them wait. My hands are clammy. I can feel a panic attack lurking beneath the surface.

Already, it's a dark night of the soul. All positive momentum to return home seems stalled. Modern day, the pandemic is rumbling through New Orleans and its densely populated French Quarter. I'm in jeopardy either place.

What if I simply finish what I started? I could take enough pills to do the job this time, with Marie's help, of course. Would she help me? Would Julie?

Snap out of it! I scold myself. Too much panicking. Besides, who knows if I'd be better off dead? Maybe when we think nothing else could worsen a situation, it's still better than the alternative. Modern day was better than 1862, right? Right now, I'm surrounded by filthiness and disease, lack of modern utilities and medicine. And it's wartime!

My mind is muddled. The facade I so precariously invented since my arrival is falling apart. Somehow, I self-soothe. I remind myself to smell the flowers; blow out the candles. Finally, I am calm – enough.

Julie graciously brings me a dinner plate, but I can only nibble. Too many strategies to determine. Nighttime eventually brings hard-won sleep to the point that I don't even dream. I'm beginning to wonder if Marie is smoke-and-mirrors.

The next morning over breakfast, Julie isn't as chatty as usual. In an odd way, I miss Master Avegno, who was typically joyful in the morning. I even weirdly miss his horrible habit at the breakfast table of hacking and coughing up phlegm.

Sally is due any moment and we consider ourselves unprepared. What Sally wants to tell us is the opposite of what we feared.

"Now, child," she points at me, "with Union soldiers overtaking New Orleans, it has come to my attention that you're trying to get home as quickly as possible," she tells me. "I understand and I can help."

We're in Julie's room and both of us sidle closer to Sally.

"What do you mean?" Julie asks innocently.

"I know that Marie Laveau will never let you return because you're too valuable here, under her thumb. She'll continue to pump you for information. And there's nothing you'll be able to do without her help. Her hold over you will be her insatiable appetite for knowledge and therefore power."

"How do you ... when did you ...," I mumble.

"Let's just say I listen more than I talk, and I've learned some secrets of Marie's over the years. I know she took you to the Pool of Souls. And I know you've been talking to your husband there and sometimes in your dreams. You must realize she can break off communication with him whenever she sees fit."

"But I thought, at the heart of it, she was a good person," I react.

"She is a good person. She's also done bad things, scary things. People work both ends of the good-and-evil spectrum and hers, let's say it kindly, is more balanced than others."

"Why are you helping me?" I probe. "I thought your allegiance was to Marie. Are you working with Marie on this?"

"Let's just say I know you know my secret, and I'm appreciative of you and Julie for staying mum. And ... I like you and know how miserable you are away from home, just as I would be. I've never seen the level of adoration you have for your husband.

"And thank you, Cici, for not asking questions."

"Who am I to judge?" I mean it.

After a pause of mutual appreciation, we hammer out a game plan.

"I've been thinking this through from every angle," Sally admits. "I've been thinking about anything that can go wrong. There are just a few loose ends to consider. And of course, Cici, you must know, everything could fail. You could be stuck here forever, in some new purgatory, or even die.

"Are you willing to take that chance?"

Chapter 28

Play of Shadows Cast

July 4, 1862

IT'S SETTLED. Parker and I will meet at the Pool of Souls. I'll return to him tonight. It's that simple, right?

Other than dropping off Baroness de Pontalba's dresses, Sally gives me the day off. I want to spend it walking around the French Quarter in a way that has been unavailable until now.

But it's also a dangerous time, with a captured city ill at ease. For the most part, today, the nation's Independence Day, Yankees and Southerners peacefully co-exist. Sally, Julie, and I believe the celebration of the day will provide a suitable distraction, that I can sneak into the Pool of Souls unnoticed and disappear altogether.

We would later learn just how poor the circumstances of New Orleanians were during the transition. From our isolated bubble, it doesn't seem that bad. But a gentleman who fled New Orleans for Grenada, Mississippi, told the *New York Times*: "Inflated with lust for plunder, and gloating over the prospect of filling their pockets with the rich spoils of a conquered rebel city, (Union troops) entered New Orleans to find the coveted treasures either removed to points of safety in the interior, or lying in great heaps of smoldering ashes upon the desolate levees and along the unfrequented streets ... the conquerors were baffled at every turn."

I'd later learn how very dangerous it was for me to venture into the streets, as most New Orleanians "sat gloomily at home behind closed doors, or wandered listlessly about, silent and unsympathizing spectators of passing events," the scribe continued.

"The most exemplary citizens are arrested and thrown into prison without cause, persons are taken up on mere suspicion, charged with being conspirators, tried by mock courts-martial, and condemned and executed, private property, wherever found, is seized and appropriated to the use of Yankee officers, ladies are insulted and treated with every indignity which the fiendish malignity of a brutalized New England soldier can devise. In a word, nothing is left undone, which can add to the misery and suffering of the people," wrote the gentleman, assuring readers "the stories which have been circulated in regard to the oppression and severity of Yankee rule have not been exaggerated."

Yet ignorance is bliss. It's nice to walk outside and lollygag rather than stride swiftly from one assignment to the next. Sally has kept me quite busy, acting as if it's not unsafe on the streets. When I'm not attending clients, I'm inside my room drawing sketches, making patterns, gathering skirts, even tufting pillows. Whatever it takes to earn my keep.

Even though it's partly cloudy, the heat and humidity are almost unbearable. In 2019, on July 4, the heat index reached 112 degrees Fahrenheit. I wonder what it is here. I dress in my most casual day dress, with comfortable-enough shoes, a bonnet, almost all of the underdressings, and my staple umbrella.

Venturing outside, I meander through the fairy tale-like courtyard, pausing at the horse stable to love on Zelda, who so valiantly kept me safe in those early unknown hours, and to converse with Ollie, whose bravery and confidentiality was vital that first night.

Mimi is milling around chicken coops, a great venue from which to idolize Ollie. Fortunately, I miss the crochety bloke who manhandles the horses and their groomsmen. I don't want to see him anyway. He's mean-spirited. And toxic.

Strutting through the garden is a stunning peacock, occasionally spreading its wings in full glory. When Julie and I notice the peacock is female, I call her a peacunt. We dissolve into giggles after I explain the slang definition of a cunt. Of course, peacocks and peahens fall under peafowl, but in these days of war-torn angst, a belly-jiggling laugh is therapeutic.

Julie has set up an easel outdoors to capture the peacock. The elegant, 70-inch creature should be, you'd think, easy to paint. Instead, a peacock has so many details that only the finest of realist painters can pull it all together. And the tail feathers have more hues and shades of color than most artists have available. She draws in the air as a test run.

Madame Avegno is pleased with the recent addition of the peacock to her collection, and rightfully so. For her, a peacock represents a powerful spirit animal whose positive traits are considered invaluable for guidance.

Interestingly, it has been said that peacock people, as Madame Avegno sees herself, are strong and clear about all aspects of their life choices and make bold moves without hesitation, such as relocating to Paris. Kind-hearted, compassionate, generous, grateful, and polite, they prioritize dignity, esteem, and self-respect. They learn from the past to connect with the present and future.

Julie warns me not to get too accustomed to the peacock. Madame Avegno might tire of it any day.

After making the rounds, including saying hello to frumpy, grumpy Fanny, who's hustling Mimi to collect more eggs, I start down Rue Toulouse to Rue Dauphine when Julie runs up to me. "Don't forget your bread-ticket," she says, breathing heavily while handing me a piece of paper.

Despite the sunbaked sewage riddling the French Quarter, and horse and donkey dung that stifle the senses, I proceed to 400 Esplanade, where coins are freshly minted at the U.S. Mint. I wonder if it smells like money. Silly notion. Outside, Union soldiers are playing backgammon while a menacing cannon sits in the middle of the road.

I swing back to Rue Chartres, one of the busiest residential developments in the French Quarter. There's Ursuline Convent at the 1100 block, and the Beauregard-Keyes House at 1113 Rue Chartres, home to Confederate General Pierre Gustave Toutant Beauregard. Its multicultural-influenced architecture combines a one-and-a-half story Creole cottage and its steeply pitched roof with Greek Revival features, a Palladian façade, twin curved staircases leading to a Tuscan portico, and a French garden centered on a cast iron fountain and boxwood hedges. Try as I might, I cannot tell what's going on inside. Have Union soldiers taken over the house yet?

I pass Saint Louis Cathedral, flanked by The Cabildo at 701 Rue Chartres, and The Presbytere at 705 Rue Chartres, to reach Pontalba Apartment No. 5. I drop off dresses to a proxy in Madame Pontalba's absence. I was hoping to see her before she left for Paris with her sons.

An interesting "wink, wink, nod, nod" piece of architecture stands at 617 Rue Chartres, the Bartolome Bosque. The balcony monogram, made in Spanish Colonial ironwork, was installed in reverse so the initials are read from inside the house, not by passersby.

Out of curiosity, I take a few moments to slip into the pharmacy at 514 Rue Chartres, just to see if the mad pharmacist is around. Indeed, he's wearing a brown tweed suit today and acting normal. I notice that black crow again, this time sitting on a windowsill near the front door. Five more years and his secrets will surface.

If I felt brave enough, I'd go inside for gumbo at the famed Napoleon House at 500 Rue Chartres. It was built by New Orleans Mayor Nicholas Girad and offered to Napoleon Bonaparte as a place of refuge. Bonaparte never made it here.

I stroll to the French Market. Still no Café du Monde at 800 Rue Decatur. Tujague's, however, is open at 823 Rue Decatur, with Union soldiers milling around.

Since it's daytime, I use the umbrella to hide my face while walking down Rue Bourbon, taking in sights that aren't vastly different from the bars, restaurants, and striptease clubs of modern day, though it has a significant residential presence in 1862. In lieu of mannequin legs that famously swung over Big Daddy's for decades is a live version, guaranteeing satisfaction to men with money.

When I reach Rue Saint Louis, there's Antoine's Restaurant and the Creole-model Hermann-Grima House. I turn the corner on

Rue Royal to a pink stucco bank that will later become Brennan's Restaurant and an empty spot that will later house Hotel Monteleone.

I want to ride the Saint Charles streetcar, which has been rolling since 1835. But it's connected to the Saint Charles Hotel, where Major General Butler and his lieutenants live in a state of complete isolation, exiting only when heavily guarded. Partly because drunken Union officers are a mainstay along Saint Charles Avenue, "legitimate" ladies no longer stroll down that street.

By the time I return to the mansion, I'm drenched from the heat, my throat is parched, and my feet are swollen. Ollie is there to hand me a ladle of water. Julie has retreated to her art studio, where it's slightly cooler. Despite my aching limbs, I race up the stairs to share news of my day. My body quivers with the anticipation of going home.

At sundown, as planned, Julie, Sally and I head to the Pool of Souls, taking great pains to fly under the radar. We haven't seen Marie Laveau. The courtyard is bare except for that familiar black crow perched on the highest part of the wall overlooking the domain.

Out of nervousness, I nibble on a fingernail and then chastise myself. Here I am about to embark on a journey of unknown origin and worrying about bad habits seems ludicrous.

I ask both ladies if they want to come with me. Both said no fairly quickly. This is the only world they understand.

Tears flow freely as I say my goodbyes. "Juls, thank you once again for everything you've done for me. If you hadn't helped, I shudder to think what would've happened. You saved me in many ways. I'll always treasure your friendship. My time here has helped me see life in an entirely different way. I'm humbled by the lessons learned.

"And Sally, you've been a Godsend. You trusted me, helped me find meaningful work, and used my skills in a way I never thought possible. Your workmanship is exquisite. I wish you all the best, whether you stay here or return north. I'll long remember your role in helping make this return home possible."

I hug each one deeply, then spin around and kneel on rocks surrounding the Pool of Souls. I'm ready. I peer deep into the pool, searching for Parker's reflection. Just as he's coming into focus, the weather shifts dramatically. Dust devils form beside me and quickly swell into a vortex. I close my eyes to keep out flying debris, When I reopen them, the sky has darkened considerably. Julie and Sally take cover, dragging me with them.

Suddenly, the black crow swoops to the terrace and transforms into a minacious form of Marie Laveau, in full garb, with Zombi dangling around her neck. Once again, I swear her golden turban glows.

"How dare you!" Marie screams, enraged. "Who do you think you are to take off without me? To not let me know? To not ask permission? I've made your life possible!"

"M-M-Marie," I stammer, "I never meant any harm. I appreciate everything you've done for me. I wouldn't be alive if you hadn't worked your magic. But I simply must return to Parker. I want to go home. It's been almost a year!"

"I'll decide what you do, when you do it, and how. I'm not done with you yet!"

Marie shifts her wrath toward Julie and Sally, just as rain begins pouring in thick sheets.

"Traitors! How dare you two work against me! After all I've done for you? How I've kept your secret, Sally? This is how you repay me? What's so important about helping this silly little girl anyway? She couldn't even kill herself. She's a loser! She's bringing you down!"

Having been backed into a corner, all three of us huddle under a palm tree, awaiting punishment. There's no way out. Or is there? Who can we summon that has an equal strength? No one. In a flash, I sprint to the pool and dive in. Before I have time to gain any depth, Marie uses her claw-like daggers to reel me back in and toss me toward Julie and Sally.

"You can't escape me! How dare you!"

Suddenly, Marie disappears; the skies are even angrier.

In the distance, Mimi squeals in fear.

"Mimi!" Julie exclaims. We exchange looks. "What is she doing to Mimi?"

Within seconds, Marie returns with Mimi in her clutches.

"If you don't care about your friends, maybe you'll care what I do to your little girl," Marie snarls at me.

"Whose little girl?"

"Yours, Cici. Or should I call her Izzy?"

"Izzy?" I'm blindsided. How could it be her? Am I hallucinating? Is this all a nightmare? I urge myself to wake up!

"Of course, she's yours," Marie bellows, with laughter. "Do you think you got here by chance? Hell, no! I planned it all from the start. I kept throwing bad juju at you, and you kept taking it. I knew the only way to get your attention was for you to be so despondent that you wanted to give up your life. And you did just as I suspected every step of the way."

My mind is reeling. Nothing makes sense.

"So, you set it all up, for Izzy to die, and for me to want to die?"

"It was unfortunate that Izzy was raped, and later snapped," Marie sneered. "But that's what to expect when you live in a sinful city. Remember? You brought her here, to the land of the wicked. Her death is on your hands."

I want to throw up. This is too much information to swallow. Could it be true? Could I, could we, have doomed Izzy by moving to New Orleans? To the French Quarter? I'd been warned that NOLA is a fickle mistress. If so, I crave the opportunity to permanently disappear. Please put me out of my misery!

Zombi dances around Mimi's head until she screams in terror.

"Make it stop!" Mimi wails.

"Let her go," Sally says, in a husky, determined tone. "This child has nothing to do with any of this. And let Cici go home. She's served you well."

"Oh, really, Sally? Do your friends know your secret? That you have male and female body parts?"

"We know," says Julie. I nod my head. "And it doesn't matter."

Marie lifts her shoulders and tilts her head, turning up the palm of her free hand as if to say, "whatever."

Marie tightens her hold on Mimi, who has wet herself. While Marie's attention is momentarily focused on Zombi and Mimi, the three of us come up with a plan without speaking. It's a mind meld idea. Sally will make a play toward Marie. Julie will grab Mimi. And in the split second I know they're safe, I'll dive once again in the pool.

It's a risky concept. But in the few moments of Marie's reign of terror, I did the math. I know in my bones that Mimi is Mimi, Virginie Avegno's daughter. Not my precious Izzy. Marie won't harm her.

Also, Marie is simply taking credit for the ills that drove me to the brink of madness. If she couldn't keep her own children alive, she doesn't hold that type of power. Unless she didn't want them to live. I do believe she holds the power to transform herself in a black crow. It's much more imaginative than a black cat.

Our strategy is a tremendous gamble, but I have never been more certain of the facts.

As planned, Sally lunges at Marie, who lets go of Mimi, who falls into the arms of Tante Julie.

I dive headfirst into this most unusual French Quarter portal, this time tumbling black void. The silence is deafening. I want to panic, yet a peaceful calm washes over me. I'm no longer worried about holding my breath. Or what will happen next. Maybe I'm already dead. Or dying. We all wonder what happens in our last breaths. The mystery is intoxicating.

Goodbye, cruel world.

Chapter 29

Absolution

July 4, 2020

PARKER PANICS WHEN, on a routine trip to check on me, he cannot detect a pulse. He races to call the veterinarian.

"Dr. Barkley?! I think Cici is dead. Or dying. Please come over!"

"Certainly! Give me five minutes."

Because Parker knows every second counts, five minutes seems forever. True to his word, he rings the apartment on time. Parker buzzes him in.

"What happened?"

"I don't know. She was breathing and then she stopped."

Barkley investigates and finds a pulse – a faint one. He strokes my foot for signs of brain damage. There is none.

"She's experiencing something unsettling," he says. "Has she moved or given any indication she's waking up?"

"No. She just started fading away."

At that moment, my body begins emerging from the coma. I had crossed the plane successfully. Initially, I shifted to a vegetative state, and then partial consciousness.

"Well, look who's back," Barkley tells me, shining a bright light in my eyes. But I'm not fully cognizant.

Parker practically shoves Barkley out of the way to cradle me. At first glance, Parker is concerned I'm not in my right mind because I'm dazed and confused.

"It's rare for a person to move from coma to a state of full consciousness quickly," Barkley explains, while re-checking my vital signs. "She should improve over the next few days and weeks."

Parker hugs me tightly, tears falling onto my cheeks, while he lovingly wraps me in my trusty wooby.

As almost an afterthought, Parker asks what to do about the feeding tube.

"When she's able to eat for a week without using the feeding tube and her weight is stable, then Allison can discuss the possibility of removing it."

Bless her heart, Allison stayed behind when the pandemic hit, primarily to help Parker care for me.

"Allison will also remove her catheter, but we may need to wait a little bit until her instincts kick in."

"Doc, how can I ever repay you and Allison?"

Fortunately, Barkley knows how tight money is, and declares the debt forgiven.

"I'll repay you, I will. I promise. This is worth everything!"

"Seeing her return to you is payment enough. Continue being careful when you go out. Wear your mask everywhere, wash it often, and carry your alcohol spray bottle. Avoid public places and shop when others don't. And see if you can get the POA to do something about that crazy neighbor of yours. Between talking loudly on the phone and the TV blaring, I could hardly hear myself think."

"I know!"

As he turns to leave, Barkley gives us promising news. "I heard that several pharmaceutical companies are working on a vaccine. Maybe we'll have a reprieve from the virus before too long. Hang in there. And congratulations on bringing back Cici. Call if you need me."

Parker was gone long enough to walk Barkley to the door, and then made a beeline to my bedside. I don't know how long I was incoherent, but when I was fully awake, Parker's arms were holding me tightly. We cried tears of joy, so grateful to reach this milestone. His touch, his aura, are already healing me.

It took weeks to share everything that had happened. I wondered what happened to

Marie Laveau, Julie, Sally, Mimi, and even Virginie Avegno.

"In an effort to blackmail me to stay, Marie told me Mimi was our Izzy, and that she'd planned everything that went wrong so I'd take the bait."

"That's wicked," Parker scoffs, then hugs me tighter.

Comparing notes is bittersweet because we eventually covered the plight that landed me in 1861.

"Promise you'll never do anything like that again," Parker scolds. "You should know I'll do anything I can for you. What were you thinking, leaving me?"

"I won't try anything like that again." I vow.

My journey had come full circle. Healing, I learned, doesn't always come from medicine. It comes from peace of mind, the heart, and soul.

Kevin Hines, a survivor who jumped from the Golden Gate Bridge on September 25,

2000, claimed: "The millisecond my legs cleared (the railing), the millisecond of true free fall ... (I had) instant regret for my actions."

No matter how dire the situation, it can always, always be worse. Sometimes, all one can do is hunker down until the storms pass. One has to keep breathing, even when logic dictates that all hope is lost. The sun will rise. Everything in life is cyclical. And one doesn't need others to be seen as valuable. As a wise muse told me, "Others' opinion of you is none of your business. All you can control is from the chest in." Life on life's terms, right?

I looked up my friends online and learned that Julie lived the life she wanted, staying behind at the mansion and joining an art community while painting prolifically. Mimi and Virginie Avegno sailed to 45 Rue Cambon in Paris in 1867. If anyone is looking for that address, after Napoleon Bonaparte's grandson, Emperor Napoleon III, cleaned up the once-nasty European capital, the street was renamed Rue Luxembourg.

Mimi went on to become the dominant "it" girl in Paris society until the portrait was unveiled in 1884. It remained unsold until 1916, with artist John Sargent Singer claiming it "the best thing I've ever done."

Late in life, Virginie Avegno inherited family money that had been hidden in four trunks underground at an undisclosed location, guaranteeing a comfortable life in her remaining days.

Sally returned to the nation's capital and continued her climb as the most well-respected seamstress of her time, ultimately sewing the official American flag of its day. I realize now she had confided in Marie to help her with physical problems upon her arrival in New Orleans. If a doctor had examined Sally, she might have been imprisoned, or worse. Her secret was safe until her final day.

We now live a very simple life. It suits us well. At Parker's encouragement, I began writing my story. To flee the unhealthy environment of New Orleans during the pandemic, we moved to the mountains, wow here I set up an office overlooking rolling mountaintops. It's breathtakingly beautiful. A true place of respite.

It bothers me that Marie Laveau and I parted on sour terms. Now that I've had a chance to digest it all, I recognize the multiple layers of complications. I realize she did save me, and for that, I am grateful. I think now we could have been friends, with politics out of the way.

Once in a while, a black crow comes to rest on the outside window eave, sometimes pecking at the glass as if to say hello. Its presence no longer frightens me, though I swear it gives a wink and nod before fading into the blue sky.

Epilogue

Curtains

YES, CECILIA BEVILAQUA intrigued me. She didn't disappoint. But in the end, it wasn't Cici's time.

The afternoon she dove into the Pool of Souls, I thought she was a goner. But instead of reaching for her, I grasped the hand of the one who was ready but didn't know it. Marie Laveau had quite simply pushed life too far.

I remember the look of surprise on Marie's face when I stole her away from the Pool of Souls, along with her pet Zombi. For all her flailing about and theatrical gestures, she finally let go. To many people, Marie lived until the age of 79, dying peacefully at her Rue Saint Ann cottage, and interred in Plot No. 347 at Saint Louis No. 1 Cemetery.

However, I flew them high over Lake Pontchartrain on the way to the Great Beyond.

Rumors circulated that I dropped them in the middle of the deepest waters, and that Marie summoned her powers to morph into Calypso. Because fire and water don't mix, her time with Damballa was over and her powers fizzled.

It was a good death.

Acknowledgements

Seeds of Cecilia's adventures were planted during the years my husband, Pepper, and I lived in the French Quarter, on Rue Toulouse. Following a family tragedy, we moved there to start over, learning early on it's a terrible place to do so. But we made the best of it. We explored. We investigated. We met a diverse set of people – life timers, transplants, homeless, and other actors in the world that centers on Rue Bourbon. The more we learned, the more intrigued we were. Curiosity took me down a rabbit hole of possibilities. Then I let my imagination run loose and Rue Toulouse is the result.

This book is dedicated to Cathey Aultman, who first eyed my writing talent at Seminary High School in Mississippi, during turbulent Civil Rights reforms. She held my hand when I mistakenly wrote about a town ordinance disallowing hags to run wild in the streets. I meant hogs. There were other early slips, often resulting in being called to the principal's office. I was lucky to have her develop my early talents.

Rue Toulouse would not be possible without the brainstorming sessions with my French Quarter mates –Kellye Kendrick, Ingrid Lucia, Graig Luscombe, Steve Destri, and Dawn Bourgeois. My reading committee provided precious insight and cheered me to the finish line: Sarah Henderson, Stephanie Smith, Matthew Wilbanks, Rose Catanzaro, Carley Davis, and Karen Roquand. As I wrote in my first book, *Disconnected: Deceit & Betrayal at WorldCom* (Wiley, 2003), their stock will never drop.

About the Author

Lynne Jeter is best known as author of *Disconnected: Deceit & Betrayal at WorldCom* (Wiley, 2003), named Amazon's #1 best-selling pre-order business book in December 2002.

Versatile with a compelling writing style, Lynne is a prolific writer with travel articles published in international publications -- *U.S. Airways* and *Northwest* in-flight magazines – and high-circulation domestic publications including *Southern Accents*. She was the lead essayist for the debut edition of *Biltmore* magazine, and served as travel editor for *SOUTH* magazine, named among *Literary Journal's* top 15 new publications in 2004.

Lynne has also penned thousands of articles for business publications including the *Mississippi Business Journal*, where she was twice recognized as a U.S. Small Business Administration Journalist of the Year, and earned Press Association awards for series planning, features, spot reporting and sports stories. She was among the first investigative reporters to publish an accurate accounting within an hour of the 9/11 World Trade Center tragedy, before Osama Bin Laden was officially considered the operation mastermind.

Most recently, Lynne served as the inaugural editor-in-chief for *Medical News*, a business-to-business publication for doctors and healthcare executives serving 14 markets, with focuses on clinical and business issues. She served on Florida's Telehealth Task Force, which was integral to advancing the state's telehealth reimbursement schedule.

Recently, Lynne began writing historical fiction, incorporating her trademark grit and humor in a wildly fantastic storyline. *Rue Toulouse* is her debut book in this genre.

www.ingramcontent.com/pod-product-compliance
Lightning Source LLC
LaVergne TN
LVHW041331080426
835512LV00006B/407